MAKING DOLLHOUSES AND DIORAMAS

AN EASY APPROACH USING KITS AND READY-MADE PARTS

by Robert Schleicher

DOVER PUBLICATIONS, INC.
New York

The prices quoted in this book were correct at the time of its original publication in 1980. Since that time, prices may have changed.

Front cover: Dogwood Plantation kit from Our House with AMSI Miniatures landscaping; Colonial entryway and staircase diorama by Betty Dick.

Copyright © 1980, 1990 by Robert Schleicher.
All rights reserved under Pan American and International Copyright Conventions.

Published in Canada by General Publishing Company, Ltd., 30 Lesmill Road, Don Mills, Toronto, Ontario.
Published in the United Kingdom by Constable and Company, Ltd.

Making Dollhouses and Dioramas: An Easy Approach Using Kits and Ready-Made Parts is a republication of *Dollhouses & Dioramas: Build, Finish, and Renovate the Easy Way with Kits and Ready-Made Parts*, originally published by Chilton Book Company, Radnor, Pennsylvania, in 1980. Minor corrections have been made and the section "Suppliers and Manufacturers" has been updated. The original 8-page color section (between pages 88 and 89) has been reproduced in black and white.

Manufactured in the United States of America
Dover Publications, Inc., 31 East 2nd Street, Mineola, N.Y. 11501

Library of Congress Cataloging-in-Publication Data

Schleicher, Robert H.
    Making dollhouses and dioramas : an easy approach using kits and ready-made parts / by Robert Schleicher.
        p.   cm.
    Rev. and updated ed. of the author's Dollhouses & dioramas. c1980.
    Includes index.
    ISBN 0-486-26335-5 (pbk.)
    1. Doll-houses.   2. Miniature craft.   3. Diorama.   I. Schleicher, Robert H. Dollhouses & dioramas.   II. Title.
TT175.3.S34   1990
745.592′3—dc20   90-36304
                                                            CIP

Contents

1 The Attainable Dream   1

    The Miniature Architect   1
    Where to Buy Miniatures   3
    One Inch to the Foot   7
    The Folks Who Live There   8
    A Dollhouse or a Diorama?   10
    How Much Does It Cost?   14

INTERIORS

2 Windows and Doors   21

    Cutting Tools   22
    Working with Plywood   25
    Working with Foam-Core Board   26
    Working with Cardboard   26
    Assembling Windows and Doors   29
    Adapting Windows and Doors to Interiors   30
    Installing Windows and Doors   30
    Installing Window Glass   32

3 Interior Walls and Floors   33

    Paints for Miniature Walls   33
    Self-Stick Wallpaper   36
    Molding and Wainscoting   37
    Gang-Planking and Other Floor Finishes   40
    Cut-out Carpets and Linoleum   42

4 Lights, Lamps, and Wiring   **44**

Electrical Wiring Systems   44
Lights and Lamps   46
The Miniature Electrician   47
Tape-and-Punch Wiring   49
Installing Conventional Wiring   52

EXTERIORS

5 Bricks, Stone, and Other Siding   **57**

Applying Bricks, Stone, or Siding   57
Painting the Panels   62
Real Brick Walls   63
Simplified Brick and Stone Products   64
Clapboard and Other Wood Siding   67
Board-and-Batten Siding   69
Stucco Effects   71

6 Shingles, Shakes, and Tiles   **73**

Changing the Pitch of the Roof   73
Shakes and Shingles   74
Slate Shingles   76
Spanish Tiles   78
Metal Roofs   78
Thatch Roofs   79
Chimneys, Downspouts, and Details   80
Adding Dormers   80

7 Landscaping and Exterior Decorating   **84**

The Yard   84
Porches and Patios   85
Concrete Effects   86
Landscaping the Lawn and Foliage   88
Ground Cover   89
Trees and Shrubs   91
Living Shrubbery   95

SHADOWBOX DIORAMAS

8 The One-Scene Shadowbox   **99**

The Room on the Wall   99
The Shadowbox as Furniture   102
Frames for Shadowboxes   104
Lighting   106
Accessibility   107

9 Stagecraft in Miniature   **110**

    Set-Design Basics   110
    Forced Perspective   112
    A Model of a Miniature   114
    Fred Wilson's 1880-Era Blacksmith Shop   115
    Charles Claudon's Malkata, 1453 B.C.   116
    Charles Claudon's April, 1912   119
    Betty Dick's Colonial Entryway   119

10 Special Effects   **120**

    Actors for Miniature Sets   120
    Rear-Projection Window Scenes   126
    It's All Done with Mirrors   132
    The Invisible Mirror   132
    The Infinity Box   133

DOLLHOUSES

11 Quick-Build Kits and Systems   **139**

    The Woodline System   140
    The Our House System   141
    The Handley House System   144
    The Carlson System   144
    The Northeastern System   144
    The Midwest System   146
    The Plywood Shell System   147
    Building from Plans   148

12 Dollhouse Renovation   **155**

    Reinforcing a Shell   156
    Adapting Windows and Doors   160
    Renovating Toy Dollhouses   165

Suppliers and Manufacturers   **167**

Index   **171**

1

The Attainable Dream

Whether it is a hideaway in the woods, a colonial mansion, or a Victorian townhouse, each of us has a "dream home" that we live in in fact or in fantasy. This dream house can become so much a part of our lives that, indeed, many of us consider it to be synonymous with the American Dream. And that dream can now become reality for anyone, thanks to the miniatures industry.

Just about everything imaginable for that dream house is available as a $1/12$-scale replica of full-size reality. You can buy complete kits, single rooms, or simply a salad fork for a dining-room table setting. Miniature working windows and doors and quickly applied bricks, shingles, wood siding, or interior flooring are easily fitted to one of hundreds of dollhouse kits or bare plywood dollhouse shells.

There are even quick-build dollhouse construction "systems" that can be made to fit either a preplanned design or a design of your own choosing. You have the option of locating windows and doors or even designing an entire home if you wish, or you can limit yourself to simply selecting colors and interior decor.

The Miniature Architect

Selecting a plan for building the miniature dream house and designing its interior is very similar to planning the construction and design of a full-size house. Whether you begin with a shell, a kit, or a set of plans for one of the many dollhouse construction systems, the basic house will be quite simple to build.

And one of the nicest things about the miniatures hobby is that you no longer need to be a master cabinetmaker or even a carpenter to fulfill

Fig. 1–1 This precut plywood kit by Norm's Dollhouses is a replica of a famous Victorian house in Blackhawk, Colorado.

Fig. 1–2 The prototype for the Blackhawk House kit by Norm's Dollhouses is a surviving replica from the gold-mining boom in Colorado.

your fantasy of a perfect dream house or room setting. If you can hold a saber saw, squeeze a bottle of glue, and flick a paint brush, you already have the skill that is needed to handle all of the techniques that are described in these pages. The miniatures industry has done all of the hard work and tricky fitting for you. You simply supply the imagination to turn your fantasy into a miniature reality.

Where To Buy Miniatures

Rather than going to a building supply dealer or to a lumberyard, you can simply go to a miniatures supply store, which in effect assumes the role of "contractor." Here, as a miniaturist "architect," you will be able to find the widest variety of styles for exterior trim and facades, for doors and windows, and even for landscaping your dream house. Indeed, you can rest assured that if there is (or ever was) a door, window, trim, surface finish, or detail made for a full-size house, a $\frac{1}{12}$-scale replica will be available.

Fig. 1–3 The Carlson system of kit-built dollhouses includes this unusual Tudor-styled $16\frac{1}{2} \times 22$-inch dollhouse. *Courtesy Carlson's Miniatures.*

The miniatures industry is one of those rare businesses that is primarily a "cottage industry." No pun is intended, however. The term "cottage industry" simply means that the products are made by very small manufacturers who often work in the garages or basements of their homes. There are thousands of suppliers of miniatures products, ranging from one-man or one-woman shops to giant businesses the size of CBS's X-Acto unit or Hummelwerk's Goebel Miniatures & Company.

Miniatures, dollhouse miniatures, or dollhouse components and furniture are stocked by many different retailers, from toy stores to jewelry stores to the specialty miniatures shops, of which there are several thousand, that sell nothing but 1/12-scale dollhouses, kits, components, and furnishings. But no store in the world could possibly carry every-

Fig. 1–4 This Model Homes Granny's Farmhouse has a wood front with pressed-board sides, roof, and floors, which keep the cost of the kit low. *Courtesy Model Homes, Inc.*

thing that is made for dollhouses and dioramas in 1-inch-per-foot ($\frac{1}{12}$) scale. Hundreds of the small manufacturers sell to only one or two dealers in their immediate vicinity. But if it exists in real life, it is almost certainly made in $\frac{1}{12}$ scale by someone, somewhere. Part of the pleasure of the miniatures hobby lies in locating that obscure replica or unusual window at a shop in some distant town during a vacation or business trip.

In this book I have tried to present a representative array of miniature products from both the very large manufacturers and the one-man or one-woman shops to give you a sample of what is available. It would take a catalog ten times the size of this book to show everything, and by the time it was in print, another hundred pages worth of new products would have appeared on the market.

You will see mostly Victorian items on these pages for the simple reason that that era is the most popular with miniaturists. There are furnishings on the market from many periods, however, ranging from early Egyptian to glass-and-chrome modern. The supply of miniature products is limited only by your patience in searching out the particular store that stocks or can order the obscure item you desire.

Fig. 1–5 The ultimate in the dollhouse art might be a mansion such as J. B. Lundquist's Victorian model, which is hinged for access to the rooms.

Fig. 1–6 The S/W Crafts Victorian dollhouse is an example of one of the largest of the
$^1/_{12}$-scale kits. *Courtesy S/W Crafts, Inc.*

The Yellow Pages of your telephone book is the place to start searching for suppliers of miniatures. Unfortunately, no single heading will fulfill all of your needs. The heading *Miniatures* may locate dealers in antique miniature paintings as well as dealers in dollhouse supplies. The listing *Dollhouses* includes toy stores that stock only toys, shops that cater to collectors of dolls, and sometimes the shops that cater to you, the miniaturist. A large number of retailers under the heading *Toys* carry miniaturists' supplies as well as toy dollhouses.

You must check all the *Miniatures, Dollhouses,* and *Toys* headings in the Yellow Pages in order to find all the sources of supply in any area. The listings are a bit confusing, but the search will no doubt be worth the trouble. You would be wise to contact prospective sources of supply by telephone to determine if they actually do carry supplies for the hobby of miniature dollhouses. When you visit retailers, don't be afraid to ask for something that is not displayed. Most retailers have catalogs of miniaturists' supplies that include many times the number of items actually on display in the store, and most will be happy to order something special for you, although they may require advance payment or a deposit on special-order items.

One Inch to the Foot

The miniatures hobby has been blessed with a standard scale or proportion for almost everything. The standard proportion is $1/12$ that of real life but you may also find it expressed as 1 inch equals 1 foot (that is, 1 inch equal 12 inches). It simply means that every dimension of the miniature item is exactly $1/12$ the size of the real thing. A real 7-foot (84-inch) doorway would be built in miniature to a height of 7 inches.

If you are dealing with feet, then, the notation "1 inch equals 1 foot" is a shortcut to reducing dimensions. If you find "scale inches" too confusing to figure with a conventional ruler, you can buy a $1/12$-scale ruler at most miniatures shops.

Fig. 1–7 The milled-wood sections of Northeastern's dollhouse construction system were combined with Houseworks' windows in Pete Lancaster's miniature.

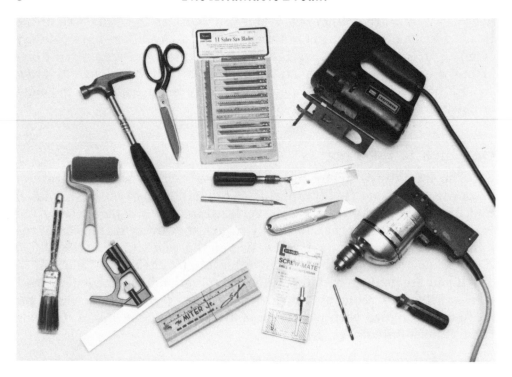

Fig. 1–8 Tools for building dollhouses and dioramas. A few power tools, such as a saber saw and drill, can make life a lot easier. From upper left: hammer, heavy scissors, finish-cut and knife-edge saber saw blades, electric saber saw, razor saw with handle, hobby knife with extra blades, utility knife with extra blades, electric $\frac{1}{4}$-inch or $\frac{3}{8}$-inch drill, screwdriver, $\frac{1}{4}$-inch drill bit, pilot bit for No. 8 $\times$ $1\frac{1}{4}$-inch wood screws, modeler's miter box, combination square, 1-inch and $\frac{1}{8}$-inch paint brushes, touch-up paint roller with refills.

The Folks Who Live There

The essence of any hobby involving models or miniatures is fantasy and imagination. The replicas that you create are supposed to be scenes as you imagine them, and they may or may not have anything to do with reality.

Many of the inexpensive toy dollhouses and furniture sets are relatively crude in appearance, unlike the more realistic miniature furniture and accessories you see within these pages. To many, that unrefined appearance is more appropriate to conveying the fantasy and recollections of their childhood. A number of imported furniture and decor items might be perfectly suitable for a re-creation of Hansel and Gretel's witch cottage or a similar fantasy scene. (Don't ask me where to find them though; that search is part of the hobby.)

The difference between three-dimensional replicas of pure flights of fantasy and true scale-model rooms or homes is also exemplified by the people who inhabit those rooms. Many miniaturists would never consider populating their rooms with dolls or figurines. For them, the hobby is designed to create environments where they themselves or their ancestors, relatives, or friends, can "live." Others prefer that the rooms be occupied by something as close as possible to a child's doll family. Those dolls can range all the way from the dried apple-head folk dolls to antique bisque china dolls to stuffed cotton-head dolls.

Still others prefer to bring life to their rooms with miniature people that are as realistic as the $1/12$-scale Chippendale furniture that surrounds them. I prefer the latter, so you will see several examples of the effect lifelike dolls can have on a miniature room setting.

If you prefer unpopulated rooms, you will find those here, too. If you are determined to see dolls in these rooms, you will simply have to duplicate the scene you like and populate it with dolls. (If you succeed in creating a dollhouse that actually attracts the Irish folk's "little people," please send me a photograph of them.)

If you want dolls for your dollhouse or shadowbox, the adults should be between 5 and 6 inches tall and the children proportionally smaller, according to their age group. Several firms offer very realistic $1/12$-scale

Fig. 1–9 Some dollhouse kits feature modular construction, which means you can start with a cottage, such as this miniature from Real Good Toys in Vermont, and expand it into a mansion. *Courtesy Real Good Toys.*

Fig. 1–10 Cottage expanded to two-story house plus attic. *Courtesy Real Good Toys.*

figures cast in plaster or resin for those miniaturists who want to create museum-quality dioramas, like some of those on these pages.

A Dollhouse or a Diorama?

When most of us think of a dollhouse, we tend to picture the rooms themselves rather than the house as a whole. That logic has created a whole new segment of the miniaturists' hobby in which a shadowbox of some kind is used to form the walls, floor, and ceiling of a single room. There is no universally accepted term for these one-room scenes. I prefer to call them what the museums call them, namely *dioramas,* but you will also see them referred to as boxes, display boxes, vignette boxes (usually large enough for only one or two pieces of furniture), showcases, miniature boxes, clock boxes (simulating gutted clock cases), room boxes, and shadowboxes.

These boxes range in size from an 8 × 10-inch framed vignette box to a 12 × 22-inch room box. Most are about 10 inches deep, although some are only 3 or 4 inches deep. Anything deeper than about 12 inches is too deep to hang on a wall unless it is a shadowbox designed to hang in a corner.

If you consider that 1 inch equals 1 foot, you will understand why these shadowboxes are limited to one room. Some miniaturists group or stack several single-room shadowboxes together to re-create a houseful of rooms on a single wall.

The traditional dollhouse duplicates both the exterior and the interior of your dream home. Miniaturists have carried that concept to its ultimate by creating landscaping near the house to add that warm home-and-garden feeling to the scene.

Some clever builders have even developed hinged houses, which open to reveal interior areas that closely match the actual layout of rooms in a real home (see figure 1–5). Most dollhouse builders are content with the traditional open-back dollhouse with its single set of stacked rooms.

Size and space limitations make dioramas especially desirable to many lovers of miniatures. There are those who would rather not have a large dollhouse in the living room, even if it does have simulated

Fig. 1–11 Two-story house with rear wing and porch. *Courtesy Real Good Toys.*

Fig. 1–12 Full mansion with tower and second wing. *Courtesy Real Good Toys.*

growing plants around it. Others simply do not have the table or floor space for a dollhouse in their apartments.

For those who want to display their miniature rooms in their homes, the shadowbox on the wall is the perfect answer. If you frame the shadowbox with one of the angled-back picture frames and paint the sides of the box to match your walls, the 10- or 12-inch depth will simply not be obtrusive.

In the Shadowbox Diorama section, I have tried to present an alternative to the complete dollhouse. You will also find a few extra tricks that can be used to make a shadowbox look even larger than it is.

If you lack the space for a dollhouse (or for two or three or four dollhouses), then you might want to consider building only individual rooms or scenes in several 1 × 2-foot shadowboxes. Each shadowbox can show a single room in the same house, or it can be decorated in widely diverse styles from different periods and can include both exterior and interior scenes.

The Shadowbox Diorama section also illustrates how some of the techniques developed by set designers for the theater can be applied to make it easier to illuminate the shadowbox and to make the relatively shallow-depth scene seem to be just one part of an entire house.

Some corner shadowboxes can be used individually or stacked to make a 5- or 6-story set of dollhouse rooms that looks exactly like a corner cupboard with an open front. Even if you do not have the floor space for a complete dollhouse, you can still build a houseful of rooms by simply hanging the rooms on the walls as individual or stacked shadowboxes.

Fig. 1–13 Dioramas can be as small as this recipe box. The boxes are available at many miniatures dealers or hardware stores.

Fig. 1–14 Unfinished furniture stores carry small boxes such as this clock case, which can be used for minidioramas or vignettes.

If you want an exterior or even a garden scene, you can duplicate them in a shadowbox diorama as well. The same wall-, floor-, and ceiling-finishing techniques that apply to the inside of a dollhouse will work inside a shadowbox.

How Much Does It Cost?

Whether you want to build a dollhouse or shadowbox diorama yourself, of whether you choose to begin with a kit or a shell, you will find that determining the costs will often be a matter of common-sense planning.

Obviously it would be impractical to buy a 4 × 8-foot sheet of plywood to make a dollhouse shell. When you consider the cost of the materials, plus the cost of the trim and accessories you would want to add, you could have purchased a ready-built dollhouse shell for about the same price. And you do not even have to cut your own plywood walls or

Fig. 1–15 This Victorian sitting room was assembled inside one of Woodline's 10 × 12-inch shadowbox kits with a mirror on the left wall.

Fig. 1–16 The value of limited-production collectible items is evident in this Model Homes number 1008 Southern Plantation kit; only 1,000 numbered kits were produced. *Courtesy Model Homes, Inc.*

cut strips of wood for handmade windows yourself, because precisely cut ones can be purchased for about the same price.

The primary advantage of the materials that are available in the miniatures shops, aside from the cost, is that those kits, shells, and components take all the hard work and drudgery out of making a complete dollhouse or a shadowbox diorama.

Once you select the kit or shell, you will be able to concentrate on the creative aspects of the hobby, allowing your imagination free reign. In other words, the work that the miniatures industry has left for you is strictly for fun.

The miniatures hobby is obviously one that requires a tremendous amount of handwork. The toy dollhouse and furniture makers shortcut a lot of the handwork by painting on the details, by molding some of the parts for the more ornate tables, chairs, and windows out of plastic instead of hand carving them, or by simply leaving off the details.

If you want a truly accurate miniature, though, you will either have to spend time making it yourself or pay someone else to make it for you. If you are not handy or a do-it-yourself person, it may be less expensive in the long run to buy ready-made or custom-made items. Most of the miniatures shops have an employee or customer who will build any type of single-room diorama or complete dollhouse you could imagine. Then all you have to do is select the ready-built furnishings for the rooms. If you find a piece of furniture that is only available as a kit, the miniatures dealer can often arrange to have the kit assembled and painted or stained for you.

The vast majority of us miniaturists fall between the extremes of buy-it-all and build-it-all. The manufacturers of miniatures products cater primarily to our group by supplying most of their items as kits or partially finished replicas.

All the hard work is done and only simple assembly or painting is required. This keeps the cost within reason and allows you to have the delightful feeling that you not only did it yourself, but that you saved some money in the process. For example, a miniature chest of drawers can sell for as much as $200 ready made, but a similar period piece in a kit may sell for as little as $15.

Most dealers also offer dollhouses as completely assembled plywood shells, so all you need to add are the exterior and interior surfaces, windows, doors, and lights. Those shells and the components to finish them generally run in the $200 to $400 range.

The biggest bargains in dollhouses are probably the kits made from one of the various systems of simplified dollhouse construction. These kits seldom have working windows with the kind of detail that the component window and door miniatures have, but they do have suitable simplified windows. A complete dollhouse kit generally runs between

Fig. 1–17 The newer toy dollhouse kits, such as Skil-Craft's inexpensive Nob Hill kit, are often as exciting as some of the custom-built houses. *Courtesy Skil-Craft Corp.*

$150 and $300, depending on the size of the completed dollhouse. There will be some additional expense in providing paint, wallpaper, and lighting.

Several of the houses you see on these pages are from kits that have been upgraded or "renovated" with better-quality doors and windows from firms such as Houseworks, Carlson's Miniatures, Northeastern, Maxwell House, and AMSI Miniatures. These components range from about $6 to $20 each, so a "renovation" can easily reach $100 in windows and doors alone.

In fact, there is virtually no limit to the amount of money you can spend on the interior of a dollhouse, and the exterior shrubbery kits sold by firms such as AMSI Miniatures and Woodland Scenics can add another $20 to $100 to the cost of a complete dollhouse.

The miniatures shop will be happy to sell you a completely assembled "renovated," painted, lighted, and finished dollhouse for something between $500, if it started as a kit, and $15,000! Obviously you do save a bundle by doing the easy work yourself.

The shadowbox dioramas are certainly much less expensive than complete dollhouses for the simple reason that the dioramas are smaller. The kit and ready-built shadowboxes available from miniatures dealers range from $12 to $75, depending on the size of the box and the quality of the materials. The appearance of almost any of these can be improved considerably with a new custom-made picture frame.

Stores that custom-build picture frames can probably make you as ornate a shadowbox frame as you could desire, with an assembled shadowbox made from ¹/₂-inch plywood, for less than $150. You will have additional expenses furnishing the box with interior walls from either ¼-inch plywood or ½-inch foam-core board (such as Handley House Mini-Board), windows, doors, flooring, and lighting.

A large Victorian living room with wainscoting, a staircase, ornate ceilings and walls, hardwood flooring, and several windows and doors could add as much as $200 to the cost of a single shadowbox. About $50 is probably a more typical figure for walls, several windows, a door, and the lighting. Table lamps, rugs, and furniture are additional items of expense for a shadowbox room diorama. Dioramas that duplicate exterior scenes, such as the Victorian porch (shown in Chapter 7) and the gazebo and garden tabletop diorama (center photo section), utilize different materials, but they cost about the same as a room interior diorama.

One of the advantages of shadowbox dioramas is that you can build your "dream house" one room at a time, including a diorama or two that depict the exterior or garden scenes. This allows you to spread the expenses over an indefinite period of time and to pay particular attention to the details of each scene as you work on it.

INTERIORS

Windows and Doors

Whether you buy them ready-made or build them yourself, one way or another you will have to install windows and doors in your dollhouse or shadowbox diorama. Instead of beginning to build from scratch, you will probably have purchased a shadowbox, either ready-built or in kit form, an assembled plywood dollhouse shell, or one of the dollhouse kits or easy-to-assemble systems described in Chapter 11. Nevertheless, all of these require, or will benefit from, the installation of detailed doors and windows.

Although some dollhouse kits include windows and doors, they are almost always relatively crude to help keep the price as low as possible. Dollhouse shells and shadowboxes do not include windows or doors at all. You will, then, have to install detailed doors and windows in most of the dollhouse kits to avoid a toylike look, and you will have to fit windows and doors to the plywood dollhouse shells and to any shadowbox diorama.

You may or may not have to cut openings for the doors and windows. Many of the dollhouse assembly systems are specifically designed to eliminate this task. The openings are achieved by simply cutting the wall slats to different lengths to allow an open space to receive the door or window. Generally, you do not need to cut window or door openings in the dollhouse shells or in the kits either. Most of these shells and kits have openings sized to fit the popular brands of ready-made doors and windows. Precut openings are, in fact, one of the primary reasons that the shells and kits are so popular with miniaturists. (If the door or window you want to use is too large for the precut opening, methods for shimming the holes to fit are shown in Chapter 12.)

You may, however, want to *add* some windows or doors to your house or shadowbox, or relocate existing windows, which will require cutting holes in wood. Walls installed inside a shadowbox diorama can be made of thick cardboard like picture frame mats, which makes it relatively easy to cut the openings. The walls for shadowbox interiors can also be made of either plywood or foam-core board. The easiest possible methods for cutting window and door openings in all these types of materials are illustrated in this chapter.

Cutting Tools

Frankly, it is much easier to cut a hole for a window or door than it is to explain how it is done. Although you do not make a hole in a solid sheet of plywood, foam-core board, or cardboard with a giant cookie cutter, there is really nothing to it when you understand the tricks.

However, you will need some power tools to do the job. You can either rent or buy an electric saber saw and a ¼- or ³/₈-inch electric drill and a ¼-inch drill bit. These power tools sell for about $20 each, or you can rent them for about $5 a day. Both are extremely useful for household repairs and miscellaneous chores, so they are worthwhile lifetime investments.

You will also need a special "finish cut" saber saw blade (like Sears' No. 2867) for plywood or a "knife-edge" saber saw blade (like Sears' No. 2873) for cutting foam-core board or thick cardboard. Both blades are included in assortments, such as Sears' No. 28576, that contain about a dozen other special-use blades. These blades make a saber saw useful for cutting just about anything.

The only other tools and materials you will need are a steel carpenter's "combination" square, masking tape, a utility knife (for cutting thick cardboard), and a pencil.

That carpenter's combination square is about the most important tool you can buy for any type of work on a dollhouse or a shadowbox diorama. The cheapest tract house in the country has vertical doors and windows and square corners. If you expect your miniature to look anything like a real house, or even like a toy house, the corners must be perfectly square everywhere, and the doors and windows must be mounted perfectly vertically in the walls.

Crooked corners and crooked windows are never charming on anything but a shack. Even the relatively crude framework and walls for the blacksmith shop shadowbox diorama in Chapter 9 are perfectly vertical and square with each of the walls. The combination square will even help you get wallpaper on straight and pictures or drapes hung properly.

A combination square such as the one shown in figure 2–1 sells for as little as $7. Buy one before you do *any* work on a dollhouse. You can

Fig. 2–1 Trace the outline of the window on the plywood. Then go over the lines with a carpenter's square to be sure the window is aligned properly.

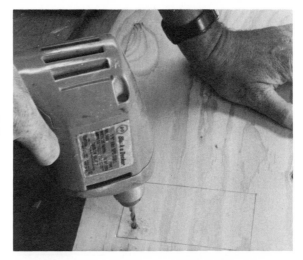

Fig. 2–2 Drill a single ¼-inch hole about ½ inch inside one corner of the window's outline.

Fig. 2–3 Cover the outline of the window with masking tape to prevent the wood from splintering along the saw cut.

Fig. 2–4 Use a finish-cut blade in the saber saw to make a smooth-sided cut in the plywood. For foam-core board, use a knife-edge blade.

Fig. 2–5 Cut along the outline to within $1/2$-inch of the corners; then swing the saw around to cut the top, the opposite side, and the bottom and cut the square corners away.

Fig. 2–6 The window should slide neatly into place. Check its alignment with the wall, using a carpenter's square.

substitute one of the simple, stamped-metal, L-shaped carpenter's squares if you would rather. The cost will be just about the same as the adjustable one.

Working with Plywood

Plywood is the most popular material for building dollhouses or for adding interior walls to shadowbox dioramas, although for adding interior walls, foam-core board or 3-ply Strathmore smooth-surface cardboard might be better choices. Plywood should be at least $1/2$ inch thick to simulate best the correct thickness or the walls of a full-size house. The interior walls of most homes are at least 6 inches thick, and this works out to exactly $1/2$ inch in the $1/12$ scale used for dollhouse miniatures.

To match the scale, exterior walls should generally be closer to $3/4$ or 1 inch thick. But $3/4$- and 1-inch-thick plywood is much too heavy for use in dollhouses. Even $1/2$-inch-thick plywood is too heavy to allow a truly portable, medium-size, two-story dollhouse. Unfortunately, $1/4$-inch plywood tends to warp unless the construction is extremely clever, like that in some of the die-cut plywood "toy" dollhouses.

If the house is relatively small, then $1/2$-inch plywood is quite satisfactory because weight will not be too much of a problem. But for constructing larger dollhouses and the interior walls in shadowbox dioramas that are to hang on a wall, a lighter material such as foam-core board, a "sandwich" of $1/8$-inch plywood and $1/4$-inch interior bracing, or one of the dollhouse construction systems illustrated in Chapter 12 would be a better choice than $1/2$-inch plywood.

If you are using $1/2$-inch plywood, buy at least a BB grade so that the knotholes will be filled on both sides of the wood. Perfectly smooth AA or AB grades are not necessary because you will be painting both sides of the plywood.

You can avoid most of the sanding with plywood if you use Norm Nielsen's technique of covering the plywood with masking tape *before* you cut it. The masking tape will prevent the wood from splintering when you make the saw cut. Using the finish-cut blade in the saber saw also helps to make a smooth cut.

Mark the window opening directly on the plywood with a pencil. The pencil mark will show through the masking tape, so you can simply apply the masking tape by centering it over the pencil line. Leave the masking tape in place until you have completely finished the work with the saber saw.

Use a carpenter's square to keep the window in perfect alignment while you trace its outline for the opening in the plywood. Then retrace the lines, using the carpenter's square as a guide to be certain that they are indeed square-cornered and perfectly straight.

Drill a $1/4$-inch hole about a half-inch inside one of the corners of the window's outline. This will allow space to insert the saw blade before beginning to cut. Cut along the pencil lines to within a half-inch of the corners; then swing the saw around to cut the top, the opposite side, and the bottom. Finally, cut the square corners away. The window should slide neatly into place.

Working with Foam-Core Board

Foam-core board is available in many of the larger artists' supply stores, and it is used in the Handley House system of dollhouse construction. The foam-core board is a sandwich of about $1/32$-inch smooth cardboard on the outer surfaces with a rigid white or beige foam-plastic inner core. The outer surfaces of the foam-core board are specially treated with a plasticlike compound to make them perfectly smooth and water repellant. The board is usually available in either $1/4$-inch or $1/2$-inch thicknesses.

Foam-core board costs several times as much as the best grades of plywood. But the primary advantages of foam core are its very light weight, its smooth finish, and the fact that is relatively easy to cut.

The Handley House book *Miniature Construction Technique to Build a Home with Mini-Board* (its name for foam-core board) is worth the price to anyone planning on building a dollhouse from foam-core board. Handley House also has a system of corners, exterior finish panels, windows, and doors for use with the foam core.

You can cut foam core with hand-held saws and knives, but it is much easier to use a knife-edge blade in a saber saw. That blade and saber saw combination allows you to work foam-core board in the same way as plywood but without the effort or the mess entailed in working with wood. The knife-edge blade will also prevent a burred edge when cutting. Foam core is not supposed to warp, but it has been my experience that it does warp at least as quickly as plywood. The obvious solution is to glue it together tightly to avoid any unbraced areas larger than about 12 × 18 inches.

Working with Cardboard

Cardboard is one of the worst choices you can make for the interior walls of a dollhouse, or even for the interior walls. Any type of cardboard will warp unless it is braced with at least $1/4$-inch-square strips of wood spaced to leave no more than a 2 × 6-inch area of cardboard unsupported. You can use it with that type of bracing for interior walls or partitions with cardboard on both sides of a framework, made like the framework for a full-size house. The Northeastern system of wall construction shown in Chapter 11 is intended to be used with its $1/8$-inch wood sheathing, but it can also be used, for interior walls, to brace cardboard.

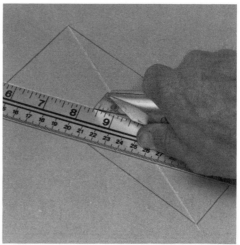

Fig. 2–7 Remove the windows from thick cardboard or from plastic wall panels by cutting diagonally across the opening with a utility knife.

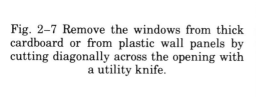

Fig. 2–8 Cut around the outline of the window very lightly; then fold back the triangles so they break off along the window's edges.

You can cut windows in plastic, cardboard, or in foam-core board using the X-cut, or diagonal-cut, technique. Simply make diagonal cuts with a hobby or utility knife through the cardboard from the opposite corners of the windows or doors. Next, cut along the actual outlines of the windows or doors and pull the triangular panels free. The diagonal cuts allow you to make precisely square corners without ripping the cardboard.

To use this method with foam core, the window or door outline will have to be located precisely on *both* sides of the foam core, because you must cut the opening from two sides, not just one. Remove the cardboard from each side and simply push out the foam interior. Actually, it is much quicker and easier to cut foam core or thick cardboard with the saber saw and knife-edge-blade method described earlier.

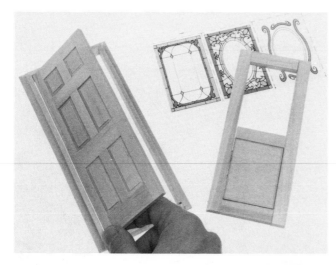

Fig. 2–9 Several brands of ready-made working doors are available, including this one by Houseworks (left) and Woodline's (right) with plastic stained-glass windows.

Fig. 2–10 Any working door can be made to swing in the opposite direction by shaving away the door sill to clear the bottom of the door.

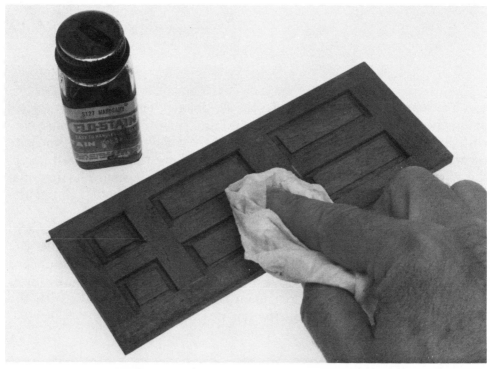

Fig. 2–11 Model-railroad shops sell small bottles of Floquil's stain for use on all types of miniature wood products.

Assembling Windows and Doors

Northeastern has a system of milled wood that is designed to duplicate precisely the construction of full-size doors and windows in $\frac{1}{12}$ scale. The dozens of different sizes and shapes of Northeastern molding are sold in 22-inch-long strips by many miniatures shops. You can use them—in the combinations shown in figure 2–12—to build a window or door of any size.

Mel's Miniatures offers completely precut kits to build doors and windows with Northeastern strips for those who would rather not bother with cutting the pieces. Mel's kits include springs along the sides of the upper windowpanes, which keep them from falling down (open), and precut clear plastic window glass. You can also use $\frac{1}{32}$-inch-thick microscope slides if you want real glass in the windows.

Northeastern has devised a system, using their milled-wood pieces, to adapt its windows or those preassembled windows sold by firms such as Houseworks, Carlson Miniatures, and Maxwell House to conventional $\frac{1}{2}$-inch walls, as well as the thinner $\frac{3}{8}$-inch or $\frac{1}{4}$-inch walls found in some of the kit dollhouses.

Fig. 2–12 Mel's Miniatures produces complete kits of precut and fitted Northeastern parts for individual windows or doors. Cyanoacrylate cement can be used for almost instant glue joints.

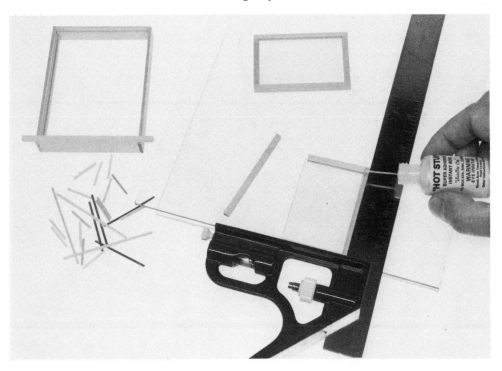

Adapting Windows and Doors to Interiors

Most of the windows and doors on the market, whether ready-made or kits, are designed to be installed in a dollhouse. This means that they include moldings for both the exterior walls and the interior walls. These windows and doors must be used somewhat differently if you want them to fit the walls of a shadowbox diorama (which usually is only a room interior).

Adapting doors to swing in rather than out is often a simple matter of shaving away the stop on a door sill of an assembled door or placing the hinges on the opposite side of a door kit. If you are using ready-made conventional "double-hung" windows, the exterior molding is usually built right into the window and the interior molding is a separate piece. You can use the exterior molding on the inside and simply omit the interior molding piece. Just remember to slide the upper half of the window down (and the lower half up) to duplicate the normal positions of the windows when viewed from inside the house.

Interior-style door handles and simulated locks are available to give authentic "interior" detail touches to the doors.

Installing Windows and Doors

The opening you have cut in the wall for the window or door is usually the key to the installation of these components. If the opening is

Fig. 2–13 Some dollhouse miniatures shops carry this Wood Works magnetic-holding jig. It speeds window assembly by holding the parts in alignment with magnetic blocks.

Fig. 2-14 Windows and doors must be in perfect vertical and horizontal alignment before they are glued in place.

not perfectly square, with truly vertical sides and horizontal top and bottom edges, proper installation may be impossible.

The goal here is to be certain that the window or door is perfectly aligned both vertically and horizontally. If the window or door itself is perfectly square, then it will automatically be aligned vertically if it is aligned horizontally.

If you are building a frame stick by stick, though, you must pay attention to all four sides of each opening. A misaligned door or window opening can be corrected fairly easily by trimming the hole just a bit larger. The frame around the window or door will hide the edges of the oversize opening.

When you are certain that the window or door you are about to install can be aligned perfectly, apply a bead of white glue, oleophatic or resin glue, or hot glue from a glue gun to the back sides of the door or window frames. Press the window or door into the opening and, again, check its vertical and horizontal alignment.

In some cases, it may be necessary to hold the window or door in place with masking tape until the glue dries. If any excess glue seeps out from beyond the edges of the frames, let it dry completely and then scrape it away with a hobby knife.

Some miniaturists prefer to paint the doors and window frames before gluing them to the walls, while others paint them after they are installed. But it is generally much easier if you paint the windows, doors, and walls *before* you glue the windows and doors in place.

Installing Window Glass

The majority of the ready-built windows and doors and the kits for these components include clear plastic to simulate window glass. The plastic has already been installed in the prebuilt windows, so you must paint around the edges of the mullions and trim, just as you would on a real window.

It is generally easier to paint even a kit-built window this way rather than painting the pieces before assembly. The paint is usually damaged by handling or coming in contact with the glue during assembly, and the touch-up can be as tedious as painting the window with the glass in place.

You can use a business card or a thin plastic credit card as a miniature paint shield to help mask the clear portion of the window while you paint the trim and mullions. This is one place where the acrylic or water-based paints can make clean-up easy and effortless—if you remove the paint from the edges of the glass with a damp rag or a damp pipe cleaner before it has dried.

If you are a stickler for detail, you might want to use real glass for your windows and for the window panels in some doors. Microscope slide glass is available in small sheets as thin as $1/32$-inch from larger drug supply firms. The glass can be scored and broken by a glass shop (or they will show you how to do it yourself) and installed like the clear plastic windowpanes.

If you happen to buy an inexpensive dollhouse or kit that does not even have clear plastic windowpanes, you can purchase plastic from most hobby shops that sell model-aircraft or model-railroad supplies. The plastic material for windowpanes can be cut with heavy scissors. White glue or the cyanoacrylate cements are best for holding either real glass or clear plastic windowpanes in place.

Interior Walls and Floors

A dollhouse or shadowbox diorama offers a unique opportunity to practice the art of interior decoration on a size and price scale that almost anyone can afford. That is one of the obvious reasons why most miniaturists become so captivated with the hobby.

You can purchase virtually anything you would want to decorate a full-size house in $1/12$ scale, including $1/12$-scale "gallons" of interior and exterior paint, wood and tile flooring, wallboard and wainscoting, and every imaginable shape of coping and trim in several different types of wood. There is even a wide selection of $1/12$-scale replicas of real wallpaper patterns and appropriate bolts of drapery and upholstery cloth with $1/12$ full-size prints and patterns.

The amount of labor required to apply the various floor and wall finishes and trim is only a fraction of the effort required for full-size interior decor. The miniatures manufacturers have thoughtfully provided flooring, wallpapers, and wall paneling in sizes that make it possible to cover almost an entire floor or wall in a single application. You can certainly use paints and wallpaper left over from decorating your own home, but before you do, take a good look at the products designed specifically for one-inch-to-the-foot miniatures.

Paints for Miniature Walls

Miniature paints for miniature walls sounds almost too cute to be practical. In fact, however, the 1-, 2-, and 8-ounce jars of water-base interior and exterior colors sold by firms such as Americolor, Model Homes, Pactra, and Polly S give the miniaturist a truly economical rainbow of colors. You cannot buy less than a quart of any of the

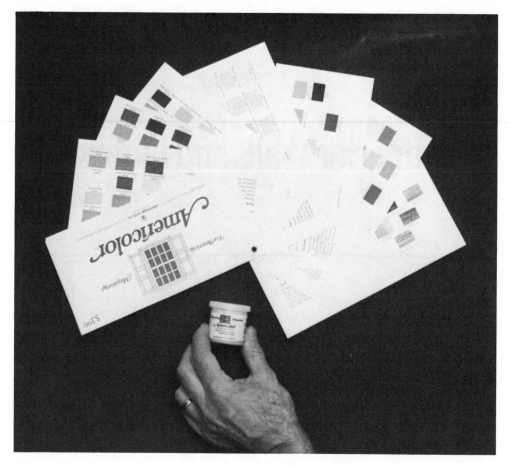

Fig. 3–1 You can buy scale-gallons of paint in an authentic shade to finish a single room.

common interior or exterior paints at conventional paint stores. And since it only takes an ounce or two for each room, those who buy by the quart tend to decorate their dollhouses in just one or two colors. This really limits the fun you can have decorating—and it looks boring, too.

The paints intended for miniaturists allow you to paint every room a different color, just as you might in decorating a full-size home. You can, of course, mix your own little bottles of paint by starting with white and adding acrylic tints. That is more trouble than it's worth for most of us, however.

The conventional paint store can be a good source of small paint brushes, and you may even locate one of the 3-inch-long "touch-up" paint rollers like that shown in figure 3–6.

To paint walls, use a paint roller, if you can find one, rather than a brush. The roller gives the slightly stippled or rough texture to the paint, which makes it look most realistic.

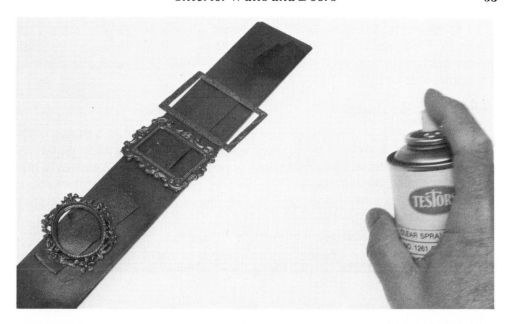

Fig. 3–2 Fold masking tape back over itself so that the sticky side can be used for holding small accessories, such as picture frames, for spray painting.

Paint stores can also supply ground walnut shells or a similar type of texture additive for paints. If you use a high proportion of the texture material to paint, you can duplicate the effect of exterior stucco or concrete. If you add just a trace of the texture material, you can duplicate the rough-finish interior plaster used in many pre-World War II homes. The stucco-type mixture can be used to duplicate the spray-on accoustical ceilings in a miniature replica of a modern room.

Fig. 3–3 Miniatures shops sell special wax to hold small objects in place, or you can use masking tape doubled back over itself.

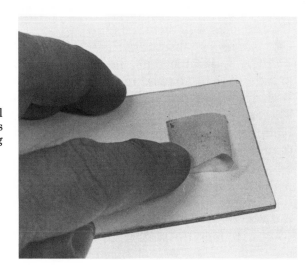

It is best to apply exterior or interior paints before you install the doors or windows. That's an advantage you would not have in a full-size house-decorating job, and it can save hours of detail painting or masking on a miniature.

Self-Stick Wallpaper

Miniaturists pride themselves in being able to find unusual solutions to common finishing problems. Self-adhesive contact paper intended for kitchen cupboard shelves is available in many patterns that look like $1/12$-scale wallpaper. The contact paper is also available in a complete selection of wood grains and finishes. Some brands of shelf paper are also self-adhesive.

The thinnest possible paper is best for use in a dollhouse. The thicker plastic-coated "papers" are difficult to mold into crisp corners, and they often have a rather large "grain" pattern molded into the surface.

You can also use some of the easy-to-apply full-size wallpapers, if you can find one with a pattern small enough for a $1/12$-scale room. Wallpaper remnants are often available for the asking at paint and wallpaper shops.

The most effective wallpapers for $1/12$-scale dollhouses and shadow-box dioramas are those that are printed especially for $1/12$-scale miniatures. Most of these wallpapers have been reduced to $1/12$ scale from actual full-size patterns. There are at least a half-dozen different brands available in a choice of fifty or more patterns, including single-color wall murals, special patterns for children's rooms, and replicas of special period patterns from Victorian and colonial times.

All of these wallpapers are as easy to apply as masking tape, if you use one of the "dries-sticky" glues such as Microscale's Liquitape or 3M Sprayment. (Model-railroad or model-aircraft shops often stock Liquitape as well as other glues, wood, wiring, lights, and other products that can be very useful to the miniaturist.)

The Liquitape must be brushed onto the wall like a thick coat of paint and then allowed to dry. It will dry sticky like tape. The wallpaper is then pressed in place to cover the entire wall, including the windows. The excess is trimmed away with a hobby knife or a single-edge razor blade. To cut the windows, use the diagonal X cut method described in figures 2–7 and 2–8 in Chapter 2.

There are also several brands of finely ground wallpaper pastes, made especially for miniaturists, if you want to apply wallpaper in the conventional manner. That touch-up paint roller is the perfect tool for rolling out any lumps in the wallpaper, regardless of what type of glue you use to hold the wallpaper in place.

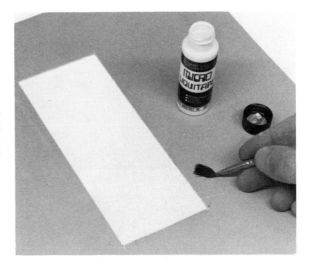

Fig. 3–4 To apply wallpaper, use an adhesive that dries tacky, such as Liquitape or 3M's Sprayment. Brush it on the wall, wait for it to dry, then press on the paper.

Molding and Wainscoting

The little details are the ones that make miniature rooms so breathtakingly realistic. And little details are exactly what fill the shelves of most miniatures shops, including every imaginable style of real wood molding.

Many of the ornate milled moldings that were common in the Victorian era are impossible to find in full-size lumberyards, but they are stocked, in $1/12$ scale, by most miniatures shops. These shops also

Fig. 3–5 Cover the entire wall, including the window areas, with the wallpaper. Cut out the windows in a diagonal pattern.

Fig. 3–6 Use one of the miniature paint rollers (for touch-up work in real homes) to apply the wallpaper firmly onto the walls.

stock a variety of milled paneling to duplicate either smooth-surface or the more complex, picture-frame style wainscotings.

These details are applied almost exactly as they would be to a full-size home, except that you can use glue rather than nails to hold the trim in place. If you use white glue, you may have to stick some common straight pins through the wood to hold it in place overnight until the glue dries.

You can do the job much faster if you use one of the special quick-drying extra-thick cyanoacrylate cements intended for model-

Fig. 3–7 Glue the windows in place with white glue, and, when the glue is dry, trim away any excess with a hobby knife.

Fig. 3–8 Midwest's mahogany sheets can be used for wainscoting with its matching half-round and corner trim.

Fig. 3–9 Model-railroad shops sell small miter boxes for modelers. They make it easy to cut and fit molding and coping precisely.

airplane builders. Carl Goldberg Model's Super Jet glue is an instant-setting cyanoacrylate cement that is formulated especially for use with wood. The glue sets within seconds, so you can install coping and other trim as fast as you can cut it.

X-Acto, Suydam, and others produce special small miter boxes and razor saws that make it easy to cut coping and other trim to fit precisely into floor and ceiling corners. It is generally best to install any ceiling finish first, followed by wallpaper or paint, and finally the flooring. Wainscoting and floor or ceiling coping should always be the last items added to any room.

Gang-Planking and Other Floor Finishes

The best-looking floors for most miniature rooms are replicas of real hardwood surfaces. There are three different types of genuine wood flooring available for miniaturists: scale-size individual boards, scribed sheetwood panels, and individual boards attached to 12-inch-square flexible backings.

Handley House is one firm that offers the 12 × 12-inch "gang-planking" in a choice of sizes to simulate either finished hardwood flooring or pine planks for stores or Early American decor. Handley

Fig. 3–10 You can cover almost an entire room with Handley House's cloth-backed scale-size floor panels. Hold the flooring down with white glue.

Fig. 3–11 Parquet wood flooring and imitation tile flooring are also available on cloth-backed sheets for covering almost an entire room at a time.

House and other firms also offer parquet flooring with real wood inserts in miniature room-size sheets.

A number of paper flooring patterns are also available, including simulated hardwood and various linoleum patterns. There are even some $1/12$-scale 9-inch-square plastic pieces on a flexible backing for "gang-tile" flooring for kitchens and bathrooms.

Common white glue or one of the brands of plastic resin-based glues are best for installing either board-by-board flooring or the gang-planking types of flooring. These glues require about an hour to dry, so you have plenty of time to position the flooring before the glue becomes hard. The glue can cause the wood flooring to warp, however, so you should cover the face of the floor with wax paper and hold it down with bricks or some other weight until the glue has dried for at least 24 hours.

The only disadvantage of a real wood floor is that you must sand it and varnish it almost exactly like its full-size, real-life counterpart. Fortunately, you will be sanding only a square foot or so of flooring, so there is very little work involved.

I recommend that you use one of the polyvinyl types of clear varnish, such as Flecto's Varathane, to achieve as smooth a finish as possible. You may have to sand the raw wood, apply one coat of varnish, sand the varnished surface after it dries, and apply a second coat of varnish to get a perfectly smooth wood-floor effect.

If you do not want to bother with sanding, use one of the two-part clear epoxy paints sold by craft supply shops for decoupage. You can also use the epoxy and resin intended for fiberglass boat repairs. The resins will give a clear covering that is a bit too thick to be truly realistic (the floor looks like it is covered with very clear ice), but the effect is realistic enough for rooms where most of the floor will be covered with rugs—and they do save a lot of time and effort.

Cut-Out Carpets and Linoleum

Carpet and linoleum shops often have catalogs that offer full-page illustrations of carpet or linoleum patterns. You may even be able to obtain obsolete pattern catalogs from a local floor-covering dealer. Bookstores often have "remainder" or bargain books with full-color illustrations of Persian or Oriental carpets on sale for as little as $4.00.

Just one such book can provide enough full-color carpets to cover the floors of several dollhouses, and the illustrations are generally about $1/12$ scale. A full-page illustration of a carpet, for instance, can measure about 8 × 10 inches, which is the precise size of an 8 × 10-*foot* carpet in $1/12$ scale.

Fig. 3–12 Full-color carpet illustrations from used books or carpet catalogs can be cut out and the edges colored with a felt-tip pen.

The carpet or linoleum is cut from the catalog and fitted to the miniature floor. You can hide the "paper" appearance by coloring the white edges with a felt-tip marking pen.

The glossy surface of paper rugs can be disguised by spraying the carpet with Testors' Dullcote clear, flat-finish spray paint. Paper linoleum can be protected with several light spray-on coats of Flecto's Varathane or Testors' Glosscote clear gloss paint.

If you search through magazines with illustrations of rooms in full-size homes, you may even find color advertisements or photographs that can provide your miniature rooms with paper marble, slate, and other special floor-covering effects.

Lights, Lamps, and Wiring

Electrical wiring is one aspect of home-building that scares many people, and well it should. If you don't know what you're doing, you could suffer a deadly electrical shock. Fortunately for hobbyists, the miniatures manufacturers have come to our rescue with several different systems of dollhouse or shadowbox diorama lighting that reduce the dangerous 115-volt household electrical current to a relatively harmless 12 volts of direct current. You need absolutely no knowlege of electricity with most of the systems, and, since they are 12 volts, they don't involve any city ordinance wiring codes, as 115-volt wiring does.

These systems also provide the means for installing ceiling fixtures, table lights, and even working wall sockets and wall switches. Some of the miniature lighting systems have wires that simply plug into various connections to run current to the lights. Others use self-adhesive copper tape similar to that used along the edges of windows in buildings with burglar-alarm systems. These systems provide what amounts to "tape-on" wiring.

Unless you are an experienced electrician, never consider using Christmas tree lights or any other type of 115-volt wiring and lights for a dollhouse or shadowbox diorama. The various electrical systems designed for miniaturists are much easier to install, and there is far less danger of a shock or a fire resulting from improper installation of the wiring.

Electrical Wiring Systems

The various wiring systems for dollhouses have one feature in common: They all have a small transformer that plugs into the 115-volt

Fig. 4–1 The Chrysolite Victorian Hanging Parlor Lamp, a plastic, glass, and metal kit, actually lights with a small bulb.

Fig. 4–2 Most dollhouse lighting systems use a plug-in transformer, such as this Cir-Kit unit, to reduce the current to 12 volts. The Cir-Kit starter kit includes a test light and a simple punch to install the brads properly for good electrical contact.

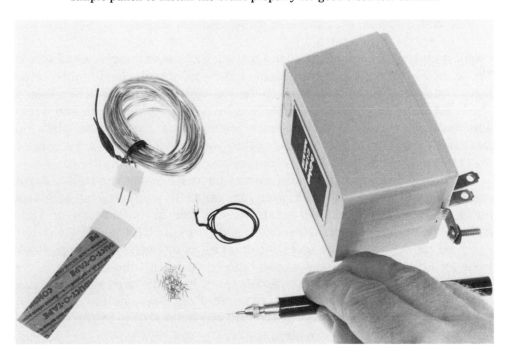

wall outlet in your home to convert that current to 12 volts of direct current. The better systems also include a fuse so that any short circuits in the 12-volt system will not damage the transformer. Many of the systems have a plug that allows you to disconnect the transformer from the dollhouse or diorama (see figure 4–7).

The differences between the various systems of miniature lighting lie in how they carry the 12 volts to each lamp or wall socket. About half of the systems use actual wires and a type of socket that permits the wires to be plugged into a terminal strip or block, so there is no soldering or other type of complex wire connection. The other miniature wiring systems use the plastic-covered, self-adhesive copper tape to carry the current to the individual lamps. The two paper-thin strips of copper beneath the tape take the place of the two solid or stranded wires in conventional wiring systems.

The various miniature lamps or light-bulb sockets generally have two very small copper wires that must be connected to the wires or copper tape of the wiring system. Some of the tape systems use tiny brass brads to connect the lamp wires to the copper tape, and others, such as Mueller Miniatures Elect-A-Lite and E-Z-Lectric, have special little plugs and even miniature "extension cords."

Cir-Kit Concepts has a clever set of scale-size wall outlets and plugs that can be used for visible wiring of table lamps. Cir-Kit also has a wall switch in $1/12$ scale that can be used to turn the lights on or off.

Lights and Lamps

A wide choice of scale-size table lamps, ceiling lights, or wall fixtures are available with 12-volt bulbs. At least one example of almost every imaginable type of full-size lighting fixture or lamp is available in $1/12$ scale. However, very few of these have easily replaceable bulbs. Most have the type of light bulb with the wires molded right into the glass. If the bulb burns out, you must replace it by removing both bulb and wires. The bulbs generally last for years; nevertheless, you must plan the installation of the lights and lamps so you can reach the wire connections without tearing out the wallpaper or ripping down walls.

A few scale-size lamps and fixtures have screw-in type bulbs. If you are concerned about bulb life, you can generally convert the wire-type bulbs to screw-in types. Alternately, you can fit each lamp or light fixture with plug-in electrical sockets and plugs such as those by Cir-Kit.

You must plan for the installation of all your lights and lamps (or at least for all your plugs and sockets) before you install the ceilings, floors, and wallpaper so that those coverings can hide the wiring. If you use foam-core walls or Northeastern's system of scale-size hollow walls, you can run the wiring inside the walls, but you must still plan the locations of the outlets and fixtures in advance.

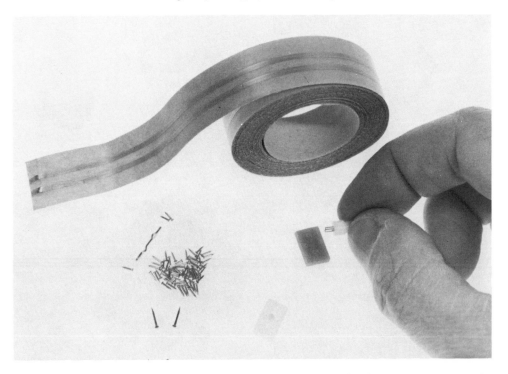

Fig. 4–3 The Cir-Kit lighting system uses copper strips inside plastic tape to carry the current. Lights are connected to the tape with wire brads or with scale-model plugs. Scale-model wall sockets (center) are also available for this system.

Dollhouse or diorama wiring is much like wiring a full-size house in that rewiring or updating the wiring often requires complete redecorating if you do it after the house is finished.

The Miniature Electrician

The various systems of wiring for miniatures allow you to pretest the locations of all the proposed lamps or light fixtures, so long as you do it before finishing the interior. It is wise, then, to buy all the fixtures and lamps, or at least all the light bulbs, that you might possibly want for each room while you are still completing work on the walls, ceiling, and floors.

You will find that you can actually decorate a miniature room with the glow from the lights just as you can decorate with full-size lighting. You may want to supplement those lamps with either indirect ceiling lighting or "imitation" outdoor illumination, as described in Chapter 8.

Remember, your full-size home receives its daytime illumination from windows facing the outside world. A dollhouse or diorama will have a maximum of two walls facing a source of natural light. There are also several methods of external room illumination suggested in Chapter 8.

Fig. 4–4 Every imaginable style and shape of ceiling light, wall light, or table lamp is available, in addition to both simple and ornate brackets to mount the lights on the ceiling.

If you want to simulate the effect of a nighttime scene with the scale-model lights and lamps as the only source of light, you may need more lights than you would first imagine. Most miniaturists find that it takes at least six light bulbs to give a realistic effect in a 10 × 15-inch room. Those six bulbs must also be distributed as evenly as possible throughout the room.

Very few full-size rooms have more than one ceiling fixture so you cannot rely on overhead lighting as a source of illumination. Even if the ceiling fixture has two or three bulbs, you will have to supplement it with several wall or table lamps.

You can increase the effectiveness of a ceiling fixture by painting the ceiling white or off-white and by using aluminum foil in the fixture to reflect the light toward the ceiling. The multibulb scale-model chandeliers can also provide a reasonable amount of light. But you will lose the warm feeling most of us want in our miniature rooms if you try to force one fixture to provide all the light for that room.

The best way to test the lighting balance in a miniature room is to obtain at least six 12-volt bulbs with 12-inch or longer wires temporarily connected to each bulb so that you can move them around. Tape the bulbs to blocks of wood to simulate table lamps or to the walls or ceilings to simulate permanent fixtures.

If possible, arrange the furniture in the appropriate places in the room so you will know where a reading lamp or wall fixture *must* be located. Rearrange the light bulbs until you get the effect you desire, and mark their locations so you will know exactly where to run the wiring or copper tape on the walls, ceiling, and floor. If you want to install on-off switches or dimmer switches on some or all of the lights, this is the time to plan for that.

Tape-and-Punch Wiring

The copper-tape wiring systems are a convenient way to run electrical current to various fixtures or lamps that are to be attached to walls or ceilings. The tape is thin enough so that it can be disguised with wallpaper, flooring, or a thick coat of latex paint.

If you mark the locations of the tape on the outer edges of the room, you can even add electrical connections after the room is completely finished. Lamps, ceiling fixtures, scale-size sockets, or wall switches can be added by simply pushing small brass brads through the tape and wrapping the fixture's wires around the brads. No soldering is needed.

If you know exactly where the copper tape is located beneath the wall or ceiling's paint or paper, you can readily plug into the electrical

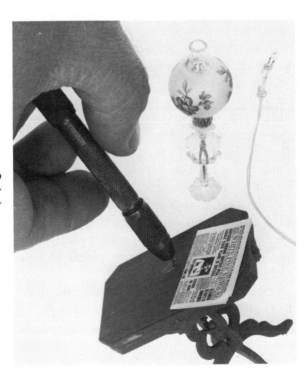

Fig. 4–5 You can hide the wires to the table lamps by drilling a $1/16$-inch hole through the table to receive the wires.

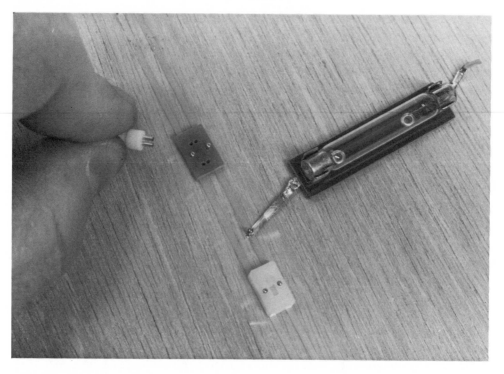

Fig. 4–6 The copper Cir-Kit tape is almost invisible on this plywood wall. The scale-model sockets, plugs, and indirect lighting units connect to the tape with brass brads.

system and add lighting. A strip of the tape all around a room just above the floor molding, for example, would allow you to locate a table lamp just about anywhere in the room without adding any additional wiring.

Cir-Kit includes a diagram to make a simple probe from two straight pins and a scrap of wood to help locate hidden wiring. The hidden wiring will be of little use, however, if it is not located near where you want extra lights, so this is no substitute for careful pretesting with light bulbs as described earlier. You must be extremely careful to avoid placing the wiring tape where you might want to pound a nail to hang a picture or mount an imitation telephone.

The tape-and-punch system of solderless dollhouse wiring is essentially a three-step wiring operation. First, the backing is peeled from the tape and the tape is pressed in place on the walls, floors, or ceilings of the dollhouse or diorama to reach the intended table lamps or ceiling lights (figure 4–7).

Second, small brass brads are driven through the tape at any intersection between two or more tapes (figure 4–8). This assures electrical flow from one piece of tape to the other. The brads are also needed to attach the lamp or light wires or to mount the Cir-Kit type of plug-in scale-model sockets or wall switches. Norm Nielsen developed a twofold system that allows you to make 90° or 45° turns with the flat tape without cutting it (and thus without using brads at the turns). His system is shown in Figures 4–9 and 4–10.

Third, the actual lamps, lights, or sockets are connected to the brads by wrapping the light bulb's wires around the brads. Then the brads are pushed firmly in place.

The most critical part of any of the tape systems is the installation of the wire brads. The brads puncture the tape, and the burrs or wisps of tape from around the hole touch the brad to make electrical contact. If there is no brad contact, there is no electrical current flow.

Cir-Kit's starter kit includes a nice little punch to start the holes in the tape. The brads, however, must, be held perfectly vertical and rigid while they are tapped down with a hammer. You can use small needle-nose pliers or tweezers to hold the brads until the last little bit is driven in.

If you bend a brad or lean it to the side, you must install a new brad at a different location on the tape *toward* the power supply, because the bent brad may have broken the copper portion of the tape. The tape may be no good beyond that point. You can sometimes patch such a break by applying a second layer of tape and electrically connecting it to the first

Fig. 4–7 Install the wiring before applying any wallpaper or wood flooring. This system has a separate plug to connect the transformer to the dollhouse.

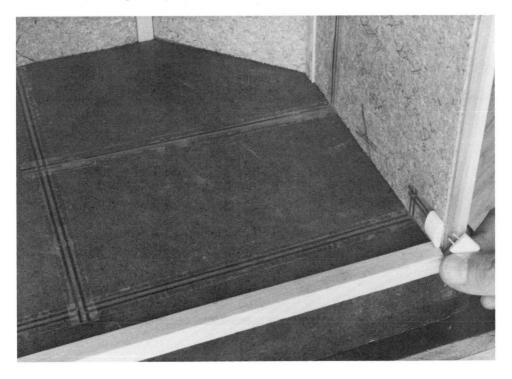

with a brad driven through each of the copper segments of the overlapping tapes.

Connect the power supply to the tape after most of it is place, but *before* applying any paint or paneling to hide the tape. Use one of the 12-volt bulbs connected to several straight pins. Jab the straight pins into the copper portions of the tape to be absolutely certain there is electrical power at every lamp location. It is much easier to trace mistakes in routing or connecting the tape before the tape is hidden beneath paint or paneling.

Installing Conventional Wiring

If you have experience in electrical wiring, it is possible to modify some of the Christmas tree lighting sets that have a transformer to reduce the voltage to about 12 volts. Do not, under any circumstances, try to modify or assemble 110-volt household lighting for a dollhouse or for scale-size lights in a diorama or shadowbox. There is just too much danger of an electrical shock, and the 110-volt bulbs produce enough heat to create a fire hazard. There might also be a danger of fire from the heat that would be generated by any short circuits.

Fig. 4–8 Pound two brass brads partially into the copper tape, wrap the bare wires from a wall or ceiling lamp around them, then push the brads firmly in place to connect the lamp into the circuit.

Fig. 4–9 You can make a 45° or 90° inter-section in the tape by making a twofold turn. First fold the wire tape in the opposite direction you want to go.

Fig. 4–10 To finish the corner turn, fold the tape back over in the proper direction.

Fig. 4–11 The E-Z-Lectric wiring system uses a transformer to reduce the current to 12 volts and small plugs and sockets on extension cords to run the wiring around the house. The wires to ceiling and wall lamps can be hidden behind drapes or beneath false ceiling panels.

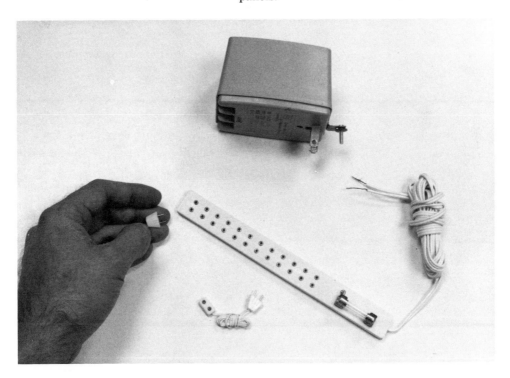

Several brands of lighting kits, including the Model Homes and Mueller Miniatures E-Z-Lectric kits, have a transformer to reduce the 110-volt household current to the 12 volts needed for miniatures. That current is also needed for most of the accessory table and ceiling lamps. The Mueller Miniatures kits include systems of plug-in wiring, and the Model Homes kits have simple twist-together connections, so you do *not* need to solder wires together.

With these conventional wiring systems, the wires to each ceiling lamp and to any wall sockets or table lamps must be routed inside the walls or ceilings. It can be difficult to hide the wires if the interior and exterior walls and ceilings are solid plywood. In some cases, the wiring can be hidden by door frames or by the kick panels or moldings that generally appear around the lower corners of the room.

If the walls and ceilings are hollow or built from foam-core board, the wiring can be located inside the walls and ceilings, just as it is in a full-size home. The wiring kits include full instructions for their installation, with specific tips on easy ways to hide the wires in the walls or ceilings.

EXTERIORS

5

Bricks, Stone, and Other Siding

The majority of the dollhouse kits and dollhouse systems include the exterior finish of the house as an integral part of the system. The unfinished plywood shells that are available from most miniatures dealers, however, do not include any exterior or interior surface finish.

Most of the information in this chapter, then, deals with how to finish the unfinished shells or how to apply exterior finishes to an "exterior" shadowbox diorama. But you may want to alter the surface on one of the dollhouse kits or finished dollhouses by installing, for example, a brick foundation or fireplace chimney.

The information on how to install windows and doors in the interior of a dollhouse or shadowbox diorama in Chapter 2 will work equally well if you are installing windows from the exterior. Exterior window frames are often more bulky in appearance than interior frames, and there are some exterior window details, such as shutters, that differ entirely from interior window treatments. It is worth repeating, though, that the well-detailed, ready-made windows can improve the appearance of any dollhouse kit or shell. And remember that the surface finishes and painting on the exterior walls should be completed before gluing any windows in place.

Applying Bricks, Stone, or Siding

There are at least a half-dozen different methods of simulating bricks on a dollhouse, including the use of genuine scale-size bricks and mortar. The easiest brick facings to apply are those that have the shapes of the bricks and mortar molded into large sheets of plastic or paper-mache. These brick sheets, from firms such as Holgate & Reynolds,

57

Handley House, and Doreen Sinnett Designs, can be applied to exterior walls much like wallpaper is applied to interior walls.

The plastic or paper-mache sheets are much stiffer than wallpaper, however, and so they are more difficult to fit in small places, or around chimneys, for example. So it is best to make paper patterns first. Most grocery stores have rolls of common white butcher paper, which is a fine material for making wall-size patterns. Some stationery stores sell large sheets or rolls of newsprint paper, which works just as well as butcher paper.

Fit and cut the butcher paper or newsprint precisely. It is far better and cheaper to make your mistakes with newsprint and use a fresh piece of paper to correct them than to have to start all over with molded wall panels. If you use butcher paper or newsprint patterns, you should then be able to fit plastic or paper-mache exterior wall panels precisely. There are several varieties of plastic and paper-mache stone, shingles, and siding that are applied in the same manner as sheets of brick, so this is a technique well worth perfecting.

The areas around doors or windows may require special treatment if you are trying to duplicate either a brick or a stone exterior wall surface. In many real-life houses, the surfaces above the windows (the lintels) and below the windows (the sills) and the door lintels may be solid slabs of stone or bricks laid on edge, either horizontally or in an arch. Sometimes the brick or stone lintels or sills are covered by the wood frames of the windows or doors. Naturally they are easier to duplicate because you do not have to imitate the fancy brickwork.

If you want to duplicate the on-edge brick sills or lintels or the arched brick lintels, you will have to cut individual bricks from the plastic or paper-mache sheets and fit them to the upper and lower edges of the window or door openings. Those details must be planned when you are cutting the paper patterns for the windows and doors.

You must also consider whether or not you want the bricks or stones to be visible on the inside edges of the windows and doors to simulate a relatively thick wall. The walls of modern brick or stone buildings are usually thin enough so that the window or door moldings and frames completely cover the inside faces of the openings and the frames extend a few inches around every side of the openings. In older structures that have very thick walls, the window or door frames rest completely inside the window or door openings in the wall. It takes some very careful fitting to make the plastic or paper-mache sheets of brick of stone appear to wrap around the edges of such thick-wall models.

It is much easier to finish the thinner walls where the window or doors frames completely hide the edges of the wall surface. This type of construction also gives you a few fractions of an inch of allowable error in cutting the window or door openings in the brick or stone sheets. The frames will hide up to $^1/_8$ inch of the wall surface around the opening. If you do make a mistake in cutting the window or door openings in your exterior surface material, don't despair. You can always hide the edges with shutters and the lintels with ornate woodwork or awnings. Mistakes in fitting the windowsills can be hidden beneath window boxes full of flowers.

If the edges of the opening will *not* be concealed by the wooden doors or window frame, you should leave an extra $^1/_{16}$ inch of siding extending inside the window or door opening. That last $^1/_{16}$ inch can be trimmed flush with the edges of the opening by shaving away a sliver of the material at a time with a sharp hobby knife after the glue holding the wall panels is dry.

The instructions furnished with the plastic and paper-mache brick, stone, shingle, or siding panels usually suggest the use of contact cement to install the panels on the walls of the dollhouse. Contact cement does not allow much room for error. You should practice using the cement with scrap materials before you apply the technique to an actual wall.

The contact cement is spread over the back side of the plastic or paper-mache siding material and over the walls of the dollhouse. The

Fig. 5–1 The vacuum-molded brick panels, such as this Holgate & Reynolds product, can be colored by spray painting or brushing on gray mortar color, then wiping an acrylic brick-red color over just the faces of the bricks.

Fig. 5-2 Houseworks bricks can be applied to a entire wall at one time with its mesh-backed "walls" of scale-size brick. Remove the bricks from any window areas and install sills and half-bricks with white glue.

Fig. 5-3 Diagonal cutters can be used to cut the scale-size real bricks in halves or thirds for duplicating window or door sills or lintels or to reproduce the "binder courses" in brick walls.

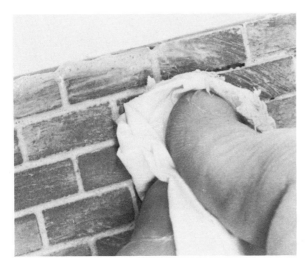

Fig. 5-4 Houseworks makes a special fine-grit mortar for use with its bricks. Simply brush it in with a stiff-bristled brush and wipe off the excess from the faces of the bricks.

cement is then allowed to dry. Place a newspaper over the walls while you position the plastic or paper-mache panels *precisely* where you want them. Hold the panels firmly in position and slip the newspaper from between the panels and the wall. The contact cement will bond instantly to itself, so you will have no time to make any adjustments.

The various types of two-part epoxy glues allow time to align the panels before the glue hardens, but they are messy to work with. Polyvinyl glues can also be used to glue plastic to wood, but the plastic must be held tightly against the wood for several hours until the glue sets. If you can devise a way of resting the dollhouse on its side, the plastic panels can be covered with an old towel and weighted down with thick plywood and full cans of paint or even cans of food until the glue sets.

The easiest way to install the plastic wall panels is simply to nail them in place with common 2d (2 penny) nails. The tiny nail heads will show, but they can be painted to match the wall. The windows and doors can be glued in place with white glue or with one of the oleophatic/resin glues, both of which will help hold the wall panels. The wall panels will bulge a bit if you use the nail system, so some type of glue is needed for perfectly flat wall surfaces.

Fig. 5–5 Joel McLeod cuts individual bricks from postcard stock to achieve the aged appearance of older brickwork (left). The bricks are then painted red, and mortar-colored acrylic wall paint is rubbed into the mortar seams (far right).

Fig. 5–6 Handley House makes a variety of vacuum-molded plastic wall panels, including this imitation shiplap or clapboard-style wall. It can be spray painted with model paints intended for plastics or brush painted with any acrylic house paint.

Painting the Panels

The imitation brick and stone surfaces molded into plastic panels by Holgate & Reynolds and Handley House are either white or light beige. They can be painted either before or after applying the panels to the walls. There are two very easy ways to simulate the colors of real bricks and mortar. I suggest you try both methods on a scrap of the paneling left over from a door or window opening.

The first method requires that the entire sheet be painted a light yellowish-gray to match the color of actual concrete mortar. This method seems to work best with the white or beige plastic sheets. When the gray paint dries, red, yellow, or gray brick or stone color is rubbed onto the surface with a rag. If you use just a small amount of paint and rub it onto the surfaces of the bricks or stones, the gray will remain visible as mortar joints between the bricks or stones.

The second method requires that the entire sheet of brick or stone be painted red, yellow, or gray to match the color you desire for the bricks or stones. When this color is dry, a mixture of about 3 parts water to 1 part acrylic paint in a yellowish-gray concrete color is brushed over the surface of the brick or stone panel. The gray will collect naturally in the simulated mortar joints. If too much gray remains on the faces of the stones or bricks, it can be wiped off while still wet with a dry rag or a paper towel.

With either method, you can achieve either a clean, new effect or an aged effect, depending on the amount of gray left on the faces of the stones or bricks.

Real Brick Walls

There are several brands of scale-model bricks available through miniatures dealers. Certainly they are the most realistic way to simulate real bricks, particularly for fireplaces or exterior chimneys, where the corners are predominant. Several varieties of actual mortar for miniaturists are also available.

The mortar, however, should not be used to hold the bricks in the same brick-by-brick type of construction used on real buildings. The individual bricks should be glued to the walls by coating about a square foot of the wall with white or plastic resin-based glue and placing the bricks on the glued surface. The wall surface must be horizontal so that the bricks will remain in place until the glue dries.

Fig. 5–7 The Handley House shiplap or clapboard siding has the seams and nail heads at the ends of the boards molded into the surface. Accent them, or create them on other paneling with a dark brown felt tip pen.

When the glue has dried overnight, any one of the special mortars can be brushed in place with a stiff brush, or you can apply yellowish-gray acrylic wall paint thickened with ground walnut shells (sold by paint stores for that purpose). Wipe excess mortar from the faces of the bricks.

Houseworks has a special wall-size (72 square inches) sheet of individual bricks that are attached to a flexible cloth mesh. The mesh can be cut to fit the sheet of bricks to any wall. The Houseworks brick sheet makes it much quicker to apply perfectly spaced bricks, and it can save a lot of time with large foundations or entire brick walls. The sheet is simply glued to the wall, and one of the miniaturists' mortars or thickened latex wall paint is applied to simulate mortar.

Individual bricks can be cut with either end-cut diagonal cutters or special tile cutters to make half-bricks for sills or lintels. Usually a "binder course" of bricks is set on edge at every twelfth horizontal row. You can add this superdetail to miniature real brick walls by cutting the full bricks into thirds and using them all along every twelfth horizontal row in place of full bricks.

Joel McLeod uses a system of cut-out postcard bricks to simulate the relatively crude shapes and sizes of colonial-vintage bricks. The same system would work just as well with slightly larger "bricks" to simulate adobe walls. Each of the bricks is cut to size in a paper cutter and glued to the cardboard or plywood walls. When the glue dries, the bricks can be painted in the same manner as the molded plastic brick panels.

Two or three layers of postcard bricks are used to simulate the ends of the bricks in sills or lintels. With the postcard system of bricks, you can simulate special brick sizes and shapes that are not available as either molded-plastic panels or as scale-size bricks.

Simplified Brick and Stone Products

Lil Brics products, from Lil Crafts, provide a system of both individual bricks cast in a special type of hard plaster and interlocking sheets of multiple-brick panels approximately 2 × 5 inches.

The Lil Bricks are precolored to simulate just about every shade of brick, including brown, pink, black, and about a half-dozen other colors. The panels are supplemented with individual scale-size bricks.

Lil Crafts also offers a special mortar mix and expanded foam-plastic interior forms for fireplaces, chimneys, and porches. The individual bricks are built around these expanded foam-plastic forms almost in the same manner as real brick would be added to a precast concrete porch, chimney, or fireplace. The multiple-brick wall panels are simply cemented in place over the walls.

Portions of panels can be installed to fill in odd spaces, and indi-

Fig. 5–8 The multibrick panels (upper right) by Lil Brik are used with its individual
bricks to make it easier to cover large surfaces quickly.

vidual Lil Brics can be used for sills and lintels. Lil Crafts mortar is then
brushed between the bricks for a perfect-scale mortar and brick effect.
The system is one of the easiest ones to use in adding exterior chimneys
to a dollhouse or shadowbox diorama.

S/W Crafts' Magic Brick and Magic Stone systems are extremely
clever means of simulating brick and stone with a simple two-step
process. First, the special plastic brick or stone mask is applied to the
area to be covered with bricks or stones. Next, a special mortarlike mix
is spread over the brick or stone mask to cover the walls or surfaces and
the masks completely. The mortar-covered surfaces are then painted to
simulate brick or stone. Finally, the mask is peeled away from the
surface. The mask will leave the indented mortar lines between the
bricks or stones.

The whole process is almost the reverse of most miniature brick or
stone systems. The bare walls form the mortar lines, while the bricks or
stones, formed by the mask, are shaped in the mortar mix. The major
advantage of the S/W system is that it allows you to apply brick or stone
textures to just about any shape or size wall or foundation—and to do so
in a very short amount of time.

Fig. 5–9 Real cement grout is smoothed between the courses of the Lil Brik bricks. The lintels above the windows and doors and the corners are made from individual bricks.

Fig. 5–10 Lil Brik offers several foam-plastic forms or cores that can be used, with its individual bricks and mortar, to make porches, chimneys, and fireplaces.

Fig. 5–11 The Lil Brik foam-plastic forms or cores have been covered with Lil Brik's individual bricks and mortar to make these two chimneys. The copper flashing where the chimney joins the roof is included.

Fig. 5–12 The core of this brick chimney is one of Lil Brik's foam-plastic pieces covered with Lil Brik's individual bricks and mortar.

The Magic Brick and Magic Stone kits include the brick or stone plastic masks, the mortar mix (ready to be mixed with water), and instructions. You must supply the paint for the mortar color and for the brick or stone colors. Latex spray paints are recommended for the mortar as well as for the brick and stone.

Clapboard and Other Wood Siding

There are at least five methods of duplicating the overlapping boards of clapboard or shiplap-style exterior siding. Handley House, for example, has vacuum-formed plastic siding sheets similar to its brick and stone sheets. Northeastern and Midwest both make scale-size wood strips that can be used for a board-by-board replica of shiplap siding or for any of the other exterior siding styles. Northeastern also offers

Fig. 5–13 This brick addition has been covered with S/W Craft's Magic Brick plastic mask and its brick texture mix. When the mask is removed, the grouting color is revealed. *Courtesy S/W Crafts, Inc.*

$3^{1}/_{2} \times 22$-inch sheets of milled basswood to simulate both shiplap and novelty siding effects.

Our House and Woodline dollhouse construction systems use walls that have shiplap siding milled into one side, with a smooth interior wall on the other. The Our House, Woodline, S/W Crafts, and several other brands of dollhouse kits also have shiplap siding as an integral part of each wall panel.

Individual shiplap "boards" can be simulated by gluing the 1-inch-wide cardboard strips intended to hide the seams of dry-wall plaster paneling to the walls of the dollhouse in a shiplap-style of overlapping boards. The cardboard strips make surprisingly realistic miniature shiplap boards because their edges are already somewhat rounded, the way shiplap boards appear after years of paint build-up. (That rounded effect can be simulated on the Northeastern or Midwest individual boards by sanding the edges.)

The Handley House plastic shiplap panels are installed using the same techniques described for its brick sheets earlier in this chapter. If you want, you can spray-paint the shiplap siding using aerosol cans of paints intended for use on plastics. Test any aerosol paint on a scrap of the plastic, because many of them will etch or warp the plastic.

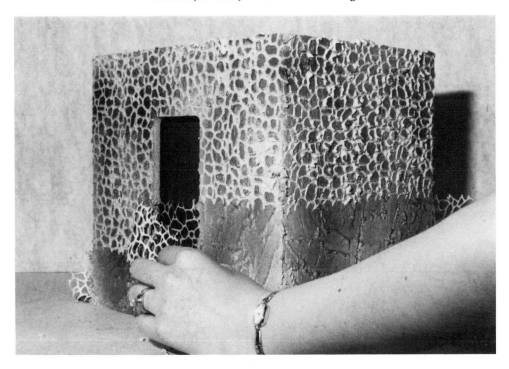

Fig. 5–14 The same mask, brick mix, and stone technique is used to make imitation stone walls with S/W Crafts' Magic Stone kit. When the stone mask is removed, only the stone shapes remain. *Courtesy S/W Crafts, Inc.*

Virtually any type of spray paint can be used on wood or cardboard, of course. It is possible to mask windows and doors with tape or paper to spray-paint the walls, but the job will be much easier if you paint the walls *before* installing windows or doors. Windows and doors can be spray painted separately, if you take the time to cover any clear windows with masking tape first.

Install any of the wood or cardboard types of shiplap or novelty-pattern siding beginning at the bottom of the walls. When you have reached about halfway up the lowest window opening, cut through the siding along the edges of the windows and break out the siding along the bottom edge. Add siding to cover the walls completely, and then cut *up* the sides of the windows and break out the siding along the upper edges of the windows.

Board-and-Batten Siding

Board and batten is the term used to describe a turn-of-the-century style of exterior wall finishes in which vertical boards were used for the wall coverings. The seams between the vertical boards were covered with small battens about $1/2 \times 2$ inches. The style is simulated by some of the aluminum and galvanized steel sidings of more modern times.

Fig. 5–15 Cardboard strips intended to hide the joints in some types of dry-wall paneling can be used to create individual "boards" on shiplap or clapboard-style dollhouse exteriors. With scissors, cut the boards to fit between or below the windows and glue them in place.

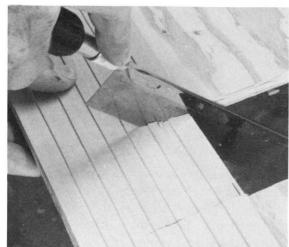

Fig. 5–16 Apply Northeastern's milled-wood panels to the plywood walls of a dollhouse shell by gluing the panels in place until they reach about halfway up each window. Cut through the panels to the bottom edges of the windows on each side.

Fig. 5–17 Carefully break out the Northeastern milled-wood paneling from the window areas. The window frame will hide the rough lower edge where the wood was broken away.

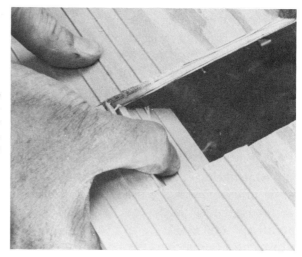

Fig. 5–18 Simple $^1/_{32}$ × $^1/_{16}$-inch wood strips can be glued in vertical rows on plywood walls to simulate the board-and-batten style for exterior walls.

You can simulate board-and-batten siding with the Northeastern or Midwest $^1/_{32}$ × $^1/_{16}$-inch wood strips glued at precisely $^1/_2$-inch intervals to a plywood or foam-core smooth-surface exterior wall. The corner trim is usually just a bit larger than the battens, so you might want to use Northeastern's milled-wood L-shape angles or some $^1/_{32}$ × $^1/_8$-inch wood strips for the corners. Similar strips will have to be used to finish the interior and exterior corners on the outside of a dollhouse with either shiplap or novelty siding.

Stucco Effects

A stucco finish is probably the easiest to use in finishing a dollhouse that has flush corners. Unfortunately, the molding trim on the corners is an integral part of many of the dollhouse kits and systems. Since corner trim generally does not appear on a stucco-finished house, some means must be devised either to sand the corner trim flush with the walls or to fill in the walls between the corner trim with thin panels.

You could, of course, use a stucco finish with one of the Tudor-style dollhouses by adding some exterior bracing and trim. For a modern or Spanish-style stucco house, it is best to start with a plywood or foam-core shell. If you are indeed trying to simulate a Spanish-style house, you

Fig. 5–19 Mix ground walnut shells or one of the other antiskid additives for boat deck
paint with regular exterior latex enamel to create brush-on scale-model stucco finishes.

might want to fill in the corners of some of the doors and windows with
half-circles of wood to give the arched effect that is common to that
architectural style.

You can prepare simulated stucco paint according to how rough you
want the walls to be. Mix ground walnut shells or one of the antiskid
deck paint additives with an appropriate pastel or white wall paint.

It is generally easier to apply the thickened simulated stucco paint
after any trim is glued to the walls and corners and after the windows
are in place. Cover the windows with masking tape and paper. The
thickened paint will flow nicely into the cavities around the window
frames and corner trim. When the "stucco" is dry, sand away any that
has spread onto the trim. Then paint the trim and window and door
frames with a brush.

You will loose much of the realism of the stucco texture if you try to
glue the windows or corner trim on top of the roughened wall surfaces.
When you apply the paint *after* the trim, the trim will look as though it
had been partially buried in the stucco, just as it would on a real house.

Shingles, Shakes, and Tiles

The roof is about the most noticeable area of most dollhouses. It is what most of us see first when the dollhouse is displayed on the floor or on a low table. You can improve the appearance of any dollhouse, then, by paying particular attention to the proper finish and design of the roof.

Changing the Pitch of the Roof

The shape, size, and style of the roof can have a profound effect on the character of the dollhouse. For example, peaked and steeply sloped roofs lend a Victorian or Tudor appearance to a house, while very shallow roof lines give a modern or Spanish appearance. The windows, doors, and trim will certainly complete the specific character of a particular style dollhouse, but the roof's pitch must be correct if those details are to have the intended effect. You can make a change in the roof pitch to modify the style of almost any dollhouse shell or kit and complete the effect when you install new windows and finish the exterior surfaces and trim.

The appearance of a dollhouse can also be altered by extending the eaves or edges of the roofs beyond the walls. Another inch or so of roof overhang on each side can make most dollhouses appear to be larger than they really are, without taking up an appreciably larger amount of floor space. (The area around a dollhouse with extended eaves can best be filled with exterior landscaping, as outlined in Chapter 7.) In fact, one of the faults that most dollhouse shells and kits share is that they lack a proper amount of roof overhang. In this case, you will have to exercise some artistic license and extend the roof somewhat beyond what might be a true-to-scale overhang.

73

In some dollhouses the windows and doors have been located too close to the tops of all of the walls, and this flaw will be even more apparent when the roof overhang is extended. It is usually possible to add another inch to the height of the upper-story walls by cutting off the peaks and splicing in pieces of 1-inch-wide board to match the thickness of the original walls. The roof peaks must be glued back in place to complete the wall-stretching.

Shakes and Shingles

Although it is unusual to see shingled exterior walls on a dollhouse, the effect can be extremely charming, particularly on a Victorian or New England style dollhouse. And as you might imagine, there are just about as many products for shake or shingle dollhouse roofs or walls as there are for the roofs of real houses.

Your miniatures shop should be able to order individual shake shingles, strips of shingles in both conventional square-end patterns, and "fish-scale" or diagonal/sawtooth patterns. The strips of shingles may be made of genuine wood, or they may be scale-size "tarpaper-and-gravel" imitation shingles.

Using strips allows you to install as much as 6 inches of each row of shingles at a time. The strips also help you to align the shingles properly. It is best, however, to begin by carefully marking perfectly parallel pencil lines across the roof to match the *length* of the shingles. Always use the pencil lines, rather than your eye, to align the individual shingles or strips.

Cut the shingle strips with heavy scissors, and use the smooth edge of the strip for the first course of shingles near the eaves. When installing each course of shingles, make certain to overlap the gaps between each shingle so that they will match the patterns of shingles on real roofs. Stain or paint the shingles or shakes, or, if you want realistic shake effects, stain the shakes gray to simulate a weathered effect.

Northeastern has an unusual type of milled-wood material for simulating individual wood shingles. The Northeastern shingle strips are $3\frac{1}{2}$ inches wide, and they are glued in place up and down the roof, rather than across in the normal shingle pattern. After the strips are glued in place, the wood is sliced to create the side seams between the shingles.

Handley House has 11×18-inch vacuum-formed plastic panels, with the shingle detail molded into the plastic. The panels should be applied, as is the brick, stone, or siding panels, by cutting them to match paper patterns. Do the fitting and fiddling with butcher paper or newsprint in order to be sure that the plastic panels will fit properly the first time. Either before or after the panels are applied, they can be spray-painted, and then weathering shades of black and gray can be rubbed on by hand.

Fig. 6–1 Shingle strips, such as these real wood shingles from Woodline Products, can be cut with heavy scissors. Use the smooth edge of the strip for the first shingle course near the eaves.

Fig. 6–2 Install the shingle strips one course at a time, overlapping the gaps between each shingle.

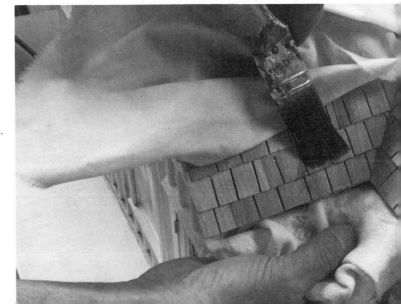

Fig. 6–3 The shingles or shakes can be stained or painted in colors to suit your fancy. For realistic shake effects, the shakes should be stained a "weathered" gray.

Fig. 6–4 Northeastern's milled-wood shingles are applied in 3½-inch-wide vertical strips. When the glue dries, slice along the grain to split off the individual shingles.

Fig. 6–5 Handley House offers vacuum-molded plastic sheets of several styles of shingles, including this fish-scale pattern. Spray paint them and rub on weathering shades of black and gray.

Slate Shingles

Fantasy Houses makes slate shingles in a vinyl plastic material that can be installed much like conventional dollhouse strip shingles. You can simulate slate shingles or slabs by painting conventional wood, card, or plastic shingles with very thick dark-gray semigloss paint.

The paint can be thickened by allowing the pigment to settle and pouring off about one-third to one-half of the clear solvent or carrier that floats on top. The paint must be thick enough so that the brush marks will still show after the paint is dry. When you brush it on, wiggle the brush back and forth to simulate the wavy texture of real slate shingles or slabs. The same technique can be used to make slate stones for porches and entryways.

Try to locate a photograph of the type of slate roof you are trying to duplicate. Some of the slate roofs on Irish cottages have shingle slabs that are several feet square, while more modern slate shingles look much like asphalt shingles, except that they have a smooth and wavy texture.

Fig. 6–6 Cut an individual row of Handley House Spanish tiles to cover the edges of the eaves. The vacuum-formed sheets can be cut with scissors.

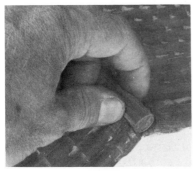

Fig. 6–7 A single ¼-or ⁵/₁₆-inch wood dowel makes an excellent ridge or roof-peak strip for Spanish tile roofs.

Fig. 6–8 Brush a mixture of 1 part dark brown acrylic paint and 3 parts water over the tiles to accent the seams and edges. You can follow up with an optional, additional "weathering" coat on the tiles of 9 parts water to 1 part gray paint.

Spanish Tiles

A tile roof is one of the most difficult styles to duplicate in miniature. Individually molded, scale-size Spanish tiles are available, but they must be installed in the same way as they are on a full-size house.

Handley House offers 11 × 16-inch vacuum-formed plastic sheets of Spanish-style tiles. Individual strips of the tiles are cut from the plastic sheet to form the wraparound side eaves that are characteristic of these types of roofs. The round tiles on the roof ridge can be simulated with a length of 1/4- or 5/16-inch-diameter wooden dowel that has been painted to match the tiles.

The vacuum-formed tiles *must* be shaded and weathered with dark brown paint so they look like the individual Spanish clay tiles. A wash of about 3 parts water and 1 part dark brown acrylic artists' paint should be brushed over the tiles after they are painted the characteristic barn red. The paint will build up on the hollow side of the vacuum-formed tiles if the dollhouse is tilted so that the peak of the roof is considerably lower than the eaves of the roof. The dollhouse must be blocked up in that position and left there until the paint dries.

Metal Roofs

One of the seldom-duplicated features of many Victorian-era homes are the metal roofs, made from either copper or galvanized iron. Copper roofs are the most striking because the copper quickly oxidizes to a mottled light green.

The metal roofs can be simulated with sheets of styrene plastic cut from "For Sale" signs. The vertical ribs that join the sheets of copper or steel can be simulated with Evergreen's 1/16-inch-square plastic strips, available at model-railroad shops. If you use 1/16-inch-square wood instead of the plastic, the wood should be painted with several coats of sealer and sanded smooth so that it will resemble metal. The greenish color of the copper roofs can be simulated with various mixtures of white and green paint.

Craft supply stores often stock paper-thin sheets of copper if you want to be bold and fit a real copper roof to your dollhouse. The copper can be polished and then protected with clear paint (flat-finish clear looks better than clear gloss), or you can actually form the green copper oxide by soaking the copper outdoors in an open container of vinegar or bleach.

This same treatment can be used for the "copper" roof-peak trim and the flashing around chimneys on a shingled roof of a dollhouse of just about any era.

Fig. 6–9 Peggy Helm Wilmoite built this English Tudor home from raw materials. The thatch roof is cut from straw placemats.

Thatch Roofs

You may want to consider adding a thatched roof to your dollhouse to make a storybook-style cottage. Architectural history books from the library will illustrate and describe the details of how a real thatched roof is traditionally made. And there is no better way to do it yourself than to follow the same steps, using either lawn trimmings or split broomstraws for the thatch. When the roof is complete, protect it with a thick spray-on coat of clear, flat-finish paint.

It is even possible to duplicate the living grass roofs of a sod house, using the imitation grass flocking sold by model-railroad shops. The pitch of the roof on most dollhouse kits or shells must be lowered for a sod house, and you must have a single-story house.

Cover the roof with about 1/4 inch of plaster and sprinkle on real dirt that has been sifted through a flour sifter. Mix equal parts of white glue and water and spray it over the dirt, using a pump-type spray bottle. Apply the imitation grass flocking. You can buy a special plastic squeeze-bottle dispenser that applies an electrostatic charge to the individual flocking strands, forcing them to stand up like grass when they contact the glue-soaked areas. You may even be able to use a flexible plastic cleanser can as a substitute for the electrostatic dispenser. This same system makes excellent grass for any exterior landscaping scenes as well.

Chimneys, Downspouts, & Details

Many dollhouse makers are perfectly satisfied to complete a kit-built dollhouse by adding nothing more than a few working windows to provide some extra realism. Other miniaturists want to add all the details that appear on a full-size house to give the exterior of their miniature as much authenticity as the interior. The roof itself must be as realistic as possible, and there is no substitute for the deep shadow effects of individual shakes, shingles, or tiles.

The cover strips for the peaks of the roofs must be applied as carefully as the shingles, shakes, or tiles. Some designs use the same materials for the roof ridge, but you can probably achieve more authenticity by forming the roof ridge from copper or aluminum strips and attaching it with Goodyear Pliobond glue. Aluminum, which comes in .016-inch-thick sheets, is available at hardware stores and can be used for downspouts, gutters, and the roof ridge. You can also cut a large disposable baking pan into $1/4$-inch-wide strips. The disposable baking pans are just about the right thickness of aluminum.

The ridge covering can also be formed from a strip of plastic cut from a "For Sale" sign and nailed in place with brads the size of straight pins. You can even use straight pins themselves, if you cut them to about $1/4$ inch with diagonal cutters held at an angle to give a sharp point.

To make rain gutters, the same plastic from the "For Sale" sign can be hand-formed over a table edge or half-round molding. Northeastern also offers a milled-wood rain gutter in $1/12$ scale, if you would rather not make your own. Downspouts can also be made from plastic drinking straws or from the aluminum or brass tubing sold by most model-airplane and model-railroad hobby shops.

Don't forget to add $1/12$-scale 2×4 boards under the eaves at the sides of the house to simulate the ends of rafters. Rafters are one of the details visible on many houses that are seldom seen on a dollhouse. If the rafters are not visible, the area under the roof is generally covered with a horizontal piece of wood and some molding both along the edge of the roof and between the under-eave wood and the sides of the house.

Adding Dormers

If your miniature house has a peaked roof and the style in which you are modeling it would allow the use of dormers, you should definitely consider adding them. Adding dormers to an otherwise empty attic area

Fig. 6–10 The rain gutters on this home are Northeastern's milled-wood shapes. The downspout is a $3/16$-inch-diameter wood dowel, which has been cut, fitted, and glued to make the elbow at the top.

can be as effective in increasing living space in a dollhouse as it can in a full-size house.

Kits and ready-made dormers are available from several miniatures suppliers, including Houseworks and Our House. You will have to cut holes in the roof to match the inside shape of the dormers, but that is simple enough if you use the saber-saw method illustrated in Chapter 2. Be particularly careful to match the size of the hole to the shape of the *inside* walls of the dormer, because the inside corners should be perfectly flush if you are going to apply wallpaper or paint directly to the inside of the dormer and roof.

If the dormer you buy does not match the exact pitch of the roof on your dollhouse, you may actually find it easier to alter the roof-pitch angle on the dollhouse itself, rather than fiddle with the shape of the

Fig. 6–11 The single dormer on the roof of Model Homes' Townhouse kit gives the miniature extra character. The dormer is included in the kit. *Courtesy Model Homes.*

dormer. It is easy enough to remove the roof and saw down the peaks of the side walls to reduce the roof pitch by a few degrees.

If you must *increase* the pitch of the roof, you may be able to block up the roof with some strips of wood cut to a wedge shape and fitted between the roof pieces and the top edges of the end walls. The wedges can be hidden beneath new corner or baseboard-style coping trim, or you might consider applying shingles to the upper portions of the end walls to cover the alterations.

If you increase the pitch of the roof by more than a few degrees, you will need longer roof panels, so be sure to take that into consideration before finishing the roof. You could cut entirely new panels or extend the existing ones with strips.

Landscaping and Exterior Decorating

Much of the charm of a full-size house lies in its landscaping, porches, sidewalks, and other external decor. You seldom see an artist's or architect's rendering of any type of building without also seeing at least a few trees and shrubs. And nothing makes the outside of a miniature home look more "lived in" than just a bit of exterior decorating.

The miniatures and model manufacturers have made this aspect of the miniatures hobby as easy as all of the other aspects providing easy-to-use methods of duplicating foliage. The few details that are not available in a miniatures or hobby shop are easy enough to locate in hardware stores.

The Yard

You will need at least a small yard area around two or more sides of your dollhouse to provide the space for landscaping, porches, walks, and fences. Generally, it is wise to mount any dollhouse on a sheet of plywood, so you can pick up the edges of the plywood rather than the basement of the house when you need to move it.

When you order the cut-to-size piece of ³/₄-inch plywood for the base of the house, why not add another 6 to 12 inches each to the width and length so that you will have space for a yard on two sides? You can get by with as little as 3 inches of "yard" on the sides or front of the house, but 6 inches leaves enough room for some yard details such as children's swings, a small fountain, or a flower garden. If you can allow 12 inches of yard area, you will have enough room for a gazebo or a formal garden.

There is really no need for more than an inch of plywood extending from the back or "open" side of the house—just enough to serve as a

Fig. 7–1 Norm Nielsen, Sr., used Houseworks doors, pillars, and brick to create his abandonded Victorian-porch shadowbox diorama.

"bumper," so viewers will stumble into the edge of the plywood base rather than hitting the edge of the roof. There will be plenty of "bumper" area in the plywood base for the front and side yard areas.

You can reduce the weight of that ³/₄-inch plywood base considerably by cutting out a rectangular hole about 2 inches smaller than the size of the dollhouse. The hole is positioned beneath the dollhouse, of course, where there is no need for the extra weight of the plywood. Usually the house just rests on its base, but you could attach it with glue and/or wood screws.

Porches and Patios

If you extend the "living space" for your miniature people to include a yard, you will also have room to consider adding on the outdoor living areas that are typical of homes of almost any era. Porch and patio

Fig. 7–2 Three inches is enough space to suggest a complete front yard. These bushes, hedges, and ground cover are made by AMSI Miniatures.

furniture is available through miniatures dealers, and the techniques for duplicating bricks, wood floors, and slate described in previous chapters can also be used to duplicate those surfaces for a porch or patio floor.

Some miniatures shops even carry replicas of wrought-iron porch posts or fences. Victorian-era fences and even some metal picture frames can be cut into triangular-shaped pieces to duplicate the effect of wrought-iron work where the porch posts join the roof. The posts themselves can be simple square wood or plastic painted to look like wrought iron.

There are also several dozen varieties of ornate turned-wood porch and porch fence posts and railings available through miniatures dealers from firms such as Houseworks and Northeastern. Hardware stores carry a variety of stamped metal and brown pressboard room-divider panels. These panels make most realistic 1/12-scale "gingerbread" for decorating porches, patios, and the peaks and gables of Victorian houses.

Concrete Effects

If you want to add concrete effects to your dollhouse, you will have to create them yourself. Unfortunately, there are no ready-made concrete patio, porch, or foundation slabs on the market.

Fig. 7–3 Full-size building materials, such as these one-inch-square ceramic tiles, can be used for miniature patios or sidewalks.

Fig. 7–4 Metal Miniatures' cast-metal Victorian wrought-iron fencing is just one of the many exterior details available to miniaturists.

Fig. 7–5 Pressed board room-divider panels can be cut into strips to make easy-to-install gingerbread trim on a porch or roof.

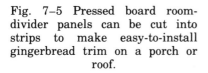

The easiest way to simulate concrete is to use 400-grit emery paper. The emery paper is cut into squares to match the size of concrete sidewalk or patio blocks or into smaller pieces to match the concrete blocks used for foundations and some patio walkways. The concrete blocks usually have a rougher texture than sidewalks, so you might want to substitute medium-grit conventional sandpaper.

The emery paper or sandpaper "blocks" are then glued to the plywood yard area, to built-up porch or patio decks, or to the foundation of the house. Leave about a $1/32$-inch gap between the pieces to simulate the expansion joints in sidewalks or the mortar joints between concrete blocks.

You will have to mix your own shade of concrete gray, starting with white latex house paint. Add a drop of black and an occasional drop of yellow until the color begins to look like concrete. Remember that the paint will fade slightly as it dries, so test your color samples after they have dried completely.

Paint the concrete areas with this yellowish-gray color and allow it to dry. Next, cut lightly into the surface of the paint and the emery paper or sandpaper with a utility or hobby knife wherever you want a crack to appear.

Now mix about 9 parts water and 1 part black artists' acrylic paint into a wash and brush the wash over the concrete. The black wash will accumulate in the gaps between the emery paper or sandpaper panels to accent the expansion seams or mortar joints, and it will collect in those knife-cut cracks. You can also rub the black around a bit to simulate the shading and dirt that gives concrete its mottled appearance.

The best way to get an effect that is as realistic as possible is to do all the painting outdoors or within sight of some actual concrete sidewalks or foundations.

Landscaping the Lawn and Foliage

There is no need to simulate a five-acre piece of ground around any miniature, even around a farmhouse miniature. You can capture the "open-spaces" effect with the back-lighted window scenes shown in Chapter 12. The only landscaping you might actually want to include around your dollhouse would be the foliage and lawn that generally appears around the front and sides of a full-size house.

The purpose of landscaping for a dollhouse or for an outdoor scene in a shadowbox diorama is to merely *suggest* the presence of an outside world. And 3 to 6-inches of "yard" is as effective as several feet for this purpose. You may need at least a foot or more of space, though, to simulate a formal garden or to house a gazebo scene. If you want to model a larger, more complex yard area, it would be wise to build the yard on a *second* piece of $3/4$-inch plywood, separate from the house and

The only illumination for this night scene "Soldier's Home, 1943" is the 12-volt bulbs in the lamps. *Photo and diorama by Charles Claudon.*

AMSI Miniatures' ground-foam foliage and shrubbery kits decorate the walls of the modified Plumbrook Cottage kit from Our House.

The bare shell of the Willoway Farm kit from Our House before painting and installation of doors and windows.

The tree in the background is real; those in the front yard of this Dogwood Plantation kit from Our House are assembled from AMSI Miniatures' kits.

You can duplicate this formal garden diorama using one of the dozen or so gazebo kits on the market and AMSI Miniatures' tree and shrub kits.

This Dura-Craft FH500 Farmhouse was assembled by Norm Nielsen exactly as outlined in the kit instructions.

The same Dura-Craft Farmhouse was "renovated" with a Houseworks bay window, an enclosed sun porch, landscaping, and other details.

The interior of Norm Nielsen's renovated Dura-Craft Farmhouse has been painted and stained to prepare it for the furnishings.

The outdoor scene behind this window is a 4 x 5-inch color transparency (slide). (The "stained glass" is a plastic insert.) You can show your own backyard in your miniature scenes using this method.

Betty Dick used an X-Acto 17½ × 11½-inch shadowbox and Real Life's Victorian Bathroom kit to create this 4½-inch deep scene.

A mirror on the left wall effectively doubles the size of this Victorian Sitting Room assembled inside a 9 x 12-inch Room Box from Woodline Products.

Shadowbox dioramas need not be limited to interior scenes. Norm Nielsen, Sr. duplicated a Victorian front porch using commercial components.

Fred Wilson duplicated a blacksmith shop interior with rough-cut ½-inch square beams and a hand-carved fireplace. The angled walls allow the use of natural lighting. Figures are almost essential for a scene such as this one. Cecil Boyd painted a Masterpiece Museum Miniatures' shopkeeper to represent the blacksmith, and Pat Milhollin painted the kibitzer.

its immediate yard. The two pieces of plywood can simply abut each other.

The landscaping around the house can be as flat as the plywood board beneath it. But the realism of such landscaping will be enhanced considerably if you build up some of the area by ½ to 1 inch to represent the uneven ground that surrounds most homes. Working in plaster or paper-mache are possibilities, but they are messy and can be quite heavy.

The landscape experts at AMSI Miniatures use ½-inch-thick Styrofoam or rigid urethane foam "boards" to build the entire yard area around their houses. The foam, which can be purchased at many craft supply stores, simply rests on the plywood yard area. It is cut with a serrated kitchen or paring knife to fit tightly around the base or foundation of the dollhouse itself. This gives the effect that the house's foundation really is set in the ground. The foam can be painted with water-base acrylic paints and glued with white glue (other paints and glues may melt it).

The Styrofoam or rigid urethane foam is soft enough so that you can literally dig it out with a knife to provide wells for basement windows, sunken flower beds, or "open dirt" circles around the bases of trees or shrubs. A second or third layer of the foam can be applied along one or more sides of the house to simulate gentle hillsides or sloping ground. The surfaces of the blocks can be easily shaped with a knife to create small knolls or terraces.

Ground Cover

The first step in landscaping the lawn around a dollhouse is to create the earth and grass ground cover. After the ground cover is applied, the flowers, shrubs, and trees are placed on top of it.

The grass mats that are available from many model-railroad dealers for landscaping railroads are the most effective scale-model grass to use around a dollhouse. The most realistic and sturdy grass mats have strands of green and yellow flocking glued on to resemble individual blades of grass in almost perfect ¹/₁₂ scale. Preiser and Sander are two common brands that are available, but if you are unable to locate them, you could use the green sawdust-covered grass mats that are made by miniatures firms such as Life-Like, Bachmann, and AHM.

If you have cut Styrofoam panels for the yard areas around the dollhouse, the next step is to cut the grass mats to fit just the "grass" areas. It will be worth the trouble it takes to fit and cut the mats if you are using the flocked mats because the effect will be so realistic.

If you are not using the flocked mats, you could simply glue on loose green sawdust or green ground foam, also available at model-railroad shops.

Fig. 7–6 The Preiser and Sander flocked grass mats are intended for model rail-roads, but they are also perfect-scale lawns for miniaturists.

You can also buy loose flocking and an electrostatic applicator, usually a flexible plastic squeeze bottle with a dozen ⅛-inch holes in the lid. (If you can get the top off to fill the container, you could try substituting an empty plastic household cleanser dispenser.) First cover the "ground" area with a mixture of 1 part water and 1 part white glue. Then spray the loose flocking onto the area with the applicator. The electrostatic charge from the applicator will force the strands of flocking to remain upright when they come in contact with the glue.

With the loose flocking, however, it is virtually impossible to match the mowed-lawn effect that is achieved with the flocked grass mats. In fact, the loose flocking will look more like a dying or crabgrass-covered lawn. If the idea of weedy areas of lawn appeals to you, you could even supplement this effect by adding weeds cut from hemp rope and glued on with white glue.

Nothing looks more like dirt than real dirt that has been sifted through a flour sifter. The dirt should be applied with the same mixture of white glue and water used to hold the "grass" in place. If you are simulating a weed-covered area, the loose dirt can be added by sprinkling it over the white glue that is still wet from the application of flocking, green sawdust, or rope-strand "weeds."

Most of us want a more formal look to our dollhouse yard areas, so the dirt that is visible should be limited to the circles around the bases or trees or bushes and to what will later become flower gardens. AMSI Miniatures sells a clean material that looks very much like dirt without actually being dirty. It is finely ground foam rubber that has been dyed brown.

AMSI, Woodland Scenics, Bachmann, and AHM all sell bags of fine-, medium-, or coarse-ground foam rubber in several shades of green as well as brown. The green works very well to simulate grass if you use the finest grind. The coarser grinds, which are about ⅛-inch across, are most suitable for simulating leaves, clumps of pine needles, or, in the bright color assortments, for blooming flowers.

Trees and Shrubs

One secret for realistic trees and bushes is to use ground foam rubber in various shades of green and in various grinds. But the foam is used for the leaves, so it is the *last* step in creating a tree or shrub. The first step is to create the trunk and branches. And remember, although grass, flowers, and shrubs can be made to exact scale, the trees should never be taller than the house itself.

Fig. 7–7 The finely ground green and brown foam from AMSI Miniatures is used to simulate grass and earth in this garden scene.

The main trunk and larger branches for any tree or shrub taller than about 6 inches are best made from the twigs of a real tree or bush. Metal trunks and branches for smaller trees and shrubs are available from AMSI Miniatures and Woodland Scenics. The metal forms are soft enough so that they can be easily twisted and bent into the various shapes of trees and bushes. The forms must then be painted brown or beige and streaked with gray or black to simulate the bark of a real tree or shrub.

The intermediate-size branches for larger bushes and trees and the entire branch system for small bushes and flowers can be made from steel wool that has been pulled apart to leave about 10 times the air space between the strands. The steel wool should be spray-painted brown.

AMSI Miniatures sells prepainted clumps of steel wool if you would rather not do it yourself. Bachmann and AHM have a synthetic woollike material for this same purpose.

Woodland Scenics' trees and shrub kits have ground foam (for leaves) already attached to a synthetic-fiber type of steel wool. This saves one step in the process of creating trees or shrubs. The brown steel wool or synthetic "wool" is stuffed in and around the trunks and larger branches to simulate the twigs and small branches of the tree or bush.

Fig. 7–8 AMSI Miniatures' landscaping materials include metal tree trunks, brown steel wool for the twigs, and ground foam for leaves.

Fig. 7–9 Living air fern can be glued into holes drilled in a straight twig to duplicate small pine trees. The fern can also be used by itself to simulate flowers or small shrubs.

Bachmann, Life-Like, Woodland Scenics, and AHM shrubbery kits and materials are sold by model-railroad stores and by some toy stores. These brands are intended for the much smaller scales of the model-railroad hobby, but they make fine $^1/_{12}$-scale bushes or very young trees, and the material works perfectly when applied to the real wood branches of $^1/_{12}$-scale trees.

The final step in creating scale-model trees, bushes, or flowers with commercial materials is to apply ground foam to simulate the leaves or clumps of pine needles. When you are satisfied with the shape of the tree or bush, spray the steel wool or synthetic wool material with an adhesive such as 3M Sprayment or AMSI Miniatures Foliage Glue.

While the glue is still tacky, sprinkle the ground foam over the glue-coated steel wool, or roll the tree or bush in a cake pan filled with the loose ground foam. That's all there is to it. If you feel that this is too much work, AMSI sells a variety of ready-built trees and shrubs made in this same manner.

If you are using Styrofoam or rigid urethane foam for the yard, the bottom of the completed trees and bushes can simply be pushed into the foam to hold them in place. If you are working directly on plywood, you will have to drill a hole for the base or trunk.

Fig. 7–10 The plastic replicas of real plants with small leaves work well in $^1/_{12}$ scale. Norm Nielsen, Sr., attached plastic leaves and branches to a real tree twig to build this scale-model tree.

Trees with wood trunks larger than $1/4$-inch diameter should be installed by drilling a $1/4$-inch hole into the trunk from the bottom. Glue a 2-inch length of $1/4$-inch round dowel into the hole; then drill a $1/4$-inch hole in the plywood to receive the dowel.

Glue the trees or shrubs in place, using a little more white glue than usual so that the excess can be pushed around the base of the trunk to simulate dirt. After the glue dries, touch it up with the same colors that were used to paint the tree trunk. Another treatment is to sprinkle on some sifted dirt or brown-colored ground foam while the glue is still wet.

Living Shrubbery

The miniaturist's $1/12$ scale is just large enough so that living plants with very tiny leaves can be used to simulate larger trees and shrubs. Some miniaturists combine the Japanese bonsai hobby of cultivating dwarf trees with dollhouse and shadowbox landscaping. Generally speaking, though, living plants are more trouble than they are worth. The one exception, however, is the completely carefree air fern. Air fern can be used as is to simulate some types of flowers, or it can be installed in $1/32$-inch holes in tree limbs to simulate the branches of pine trees.

The plastic replicas of some of the plants with tiny leaves are very well suited for landscaping dollhouses. Craft supply stores often sell several different types of plastic plants that can be used to create extremely realistic $1/12$-scale trees, bushes, and flowers. The craft stores generally have several different types of ready-made artificial flowers, as well as silk, modeling clay, and other materials to make your own. Flower making is a hobby unto itself, and craft stores carry numerous books and booklets that describe how to do it.

SHADOWBOX DIORAMAS

The One-Scene Shadowbox

Many dedicated miniaturists consider their hobby as an art form, as three-dimensional sculpture. Others, just as dedicated and enthusiastic, consider "miniatures" to be only an adult term for playing with dollhouse furniture and dollhouses. Either way, serious hobbyists at least should consider using shadowboxes to display their talents. A room full of dollhouse furniture is altered considerably when you put a frame around it. The frame draws attention to, sets off, and dignifies the display. It signifies that what is inside is of the highest craftsmanship, and it invites the observer to look closely and enjoy the miniaturist's artistry.

This can have a positive effect on your work with miniatures. If you feel you are an artist, then there is a much better chance that you will produce something that is worthy of being considered art. If you feel you are only playing with dollhouse furniture, then your work will most probably appear toylike.

That same attitude of the artist can be applied to the finishing of a complete dollhouse as well as the simple shadowbox, of course. But the shadowbox itself can make some contributions to the artistry of your work that are not possible with most dollhouses. The incredible realism and space-saving techniques described in Chapters 9 and 10 work best when applied to a shadowbox diorama.

The Room on the Wall

The primary advantage of the shadowbox, for most of us miniaturists, is that it takes up no floor space. There is a certain limitation, imposed by our families or budgets or both, on how many

99

Fig. 8–1 Betty Dick combined an X-Acto 17¹⁄₂ × 11¹⁄₂-inch shadowbox with a Real Life Victorian Bathroom kit to create this 4³⁄₄-inch-deep diorama.

complete dollhouses we can scatter around our homes. Shadowbox dioramas, however, can be placed on walls, on the shelves of bookcases, or stacked to form corner cupboards or cases of multiroom scenes. As many as a half-dozen framed shadowboxes can be grouped on a single wall, just as though they were still-life paintings.

Several shadowbox designs are intended to be stacked to become pieces of furniture in their own right. If you cannot locate one that suits you, a local cabinetmaker can assemble one for you to match the other furniture in your home. It is possible to have a hundred individual shadowbox dioramas in your home without making it look like a toy store or miniatures shop—if those shadowboxes are tastefully designed as wall-hanging pictures or as self-standing bookcase-style cabinets.

There is only one limitation to the use of shadowboxes, and that is *depth*. Most shadowboxes are 8 to 12 inches high (a single story), between 10 and 24 inches wide, and a maximum of 12 inches deep. It is simply not practical to try to hang a shadowbox much deeper than 12 inches on the wall. That same depth limitation also applies to shadowboxes that you might want to rest on an existing bookcase and to the self-stacking shadowbox/bookcases.

The only way around the depth limitation is to use the corner-cupboard design for a shadowbox, such as Fred Wilson's self-stacking units shown in figure 8–2.

Fred's shadowboxes can either be mounted on the walls of a corner, or they can be stacked as many as six high from the floor to form a corner cupboard. You could also convert some existing corner cupboards for this purpose. An example of a room built in a corner cupboard is shown in figure 9–9 in Chapter 9.

Fig. 8–2 Fred Wilson makes easy-to-assemble corner-cupboard shadowbox kits with removable front and side glass panels.

Fig. 8–3 The Wilson Works shadowboxes are designed to be stacked, if desired, to form freestanding or wall-hanging furniture.

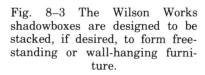

The Shadowbox as Furniture

If you are going to make shadowboxes your hobby, your first consideration must be the room in which you want to place the shadowbox, *not* the room you want to build inside the shadowbox. The shadowbox itself is supposed to be a piece of furniture for your home, not a painted plywood eyesore. So the most critical part of the shadowbox is the frame. If you are going to use shadowboxes in stacks of five or more to simulate bookcases or corner cupboards, then the frames should match the wood and the style of the other furniture in the room.

The sides of the shadowboxes should be made of a matching wood if the sides will be visible. (You might not see the sides if the shadowboxes are placed on an existing bookcase or if they are used as a corner cupboard.) You must also devise some sort of platform or legs for the shadowboxes if the designer has not already done so. A stack of five or six shadowboxes will not look like furniture unless it has something— either legs or a base—to elevate the lowest shadowbox at least 3 inches from the floor.

If you are going to place a shadowbox on an existing bookcase, then the frame on the shadowbox should either be of matching wood or of a

Fig. 8–4 The space-expanding techniques used on the stage and in films have been applied to this Victorian sitting-room diorama.

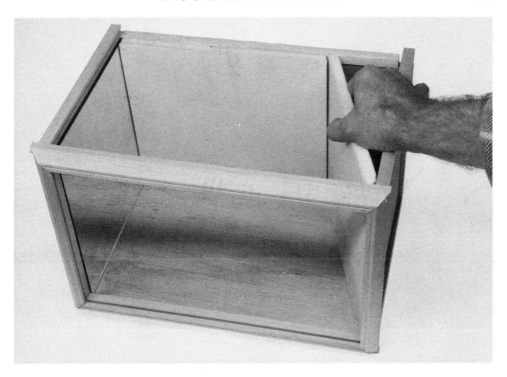

Fig. 8–5 Handley House foam-core Mini-Board was used to make the smooth corners and
walls for the Victorian sitting-room diorama.

contrasting material. The back walls of the shadowboxes are seldom
visible, so they can be made of plywood. If you are using a stack of
shadowboxes as a room divider, it is best to place two rows back-to-back
to ensure that the freestanding stacks will be completely stable. Stacks
of shadowboxes should be bolted or clamped together and, if possible,
bolted to the wall itself, so there will not be the slightest chance that
they might topple over if someone accidentally bumps into them.

Most of us will probably make only three or four shadowbox dioramas,
so the free-hanging types that look like pictures are our first consideration.
I wanted to mention the possibility of having a dozen or more shadowboxes first so you would know that very little of the hobby's pleasures
need be sacrificed if you choose to work with shadowboxes rather than
complete dollhouses.

The framed wall-hanging shadowboxes are most attractive when
only two or three of them occupy any one wall area. The picture-style
shadowboxes should be placed as close as possible to the average person's
eye level. The eye-level mounting allows the viewer to step so close to
the box that he or she can very easily imagine being inside the room.

This effect of being inside the scene works just as well when the
shadowbox diorama depicts a front or back porch, an outdoor view, or a
garden and gazebo scene.

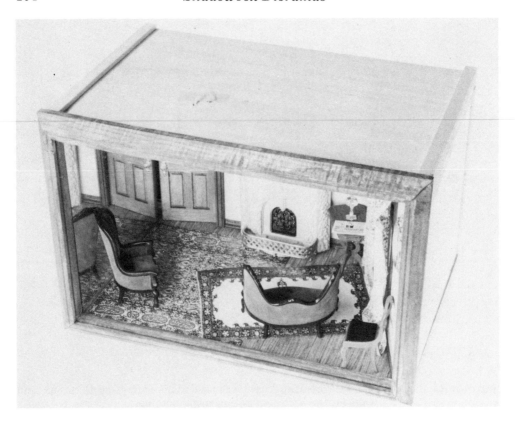

Fig. 8–6 Woodline's 8 × 12⁷/₈-inch shadowbox is about the minimum size for a single room diorama. The box is 10 inches deep.

Frames for Shadowboxes

The frame around the wall-hanging shadowboxes is just as important as the contents of the box. You may consider the frame around your diorama as the curtains on a theater stage, so long as you remember that you, like a set designer, want your audience to forget the frame or stage is there.

For the miniaturist, there are two ways to perform the "disappearing frame" trick. You can paint the frame a subdued shade of beige or brown, so it really does appear to be almost invisible, or, better, you can make the frame match the style of the full-size room, so that the viewer will leave the frame behind along with the rest of reality.

The ultimate goal of the true miniaturist should be just that—to capture the imagination of the viewer, so he or she really does feel as though the inside of the shadowbox is the *only* reality.

The frame of a shadowbox, then, must serve three distinct purposes: (1) to provide a style or decor that complements the other furnishings in the room; (2) to help disguise the fact that the "picture" is 10 or 12 inches deep, rather than the usual inch or so; and (3) to help draw the viewer's attention to the diorama in the shadowbox itself.

Obviously, you will nearly always have to compromise a bit in one of these three areas. For example, the selection of an appropriate frame can be complicated if the full-size room is decorated in Early American and the scene in the shadowbox is Victorian.

Most of the ready-made and kit shadowboxes sold by miniatures dealers have nondescript frames of simple square-cornered or beveled wood. But the scene inside any of these will be much enhanced if you add a more artistic frame to the box. Any custom framing shop can fit a picture frame of just about any style to the shadowboxes.

A custom-made frame is by far the best investment you can make to give the diorama the look of a work of art. The frame may cost twice as much as the box itself, but it is well worth it. If possible, try to select a frame material that will angle back toward the wall at the edges (a convex shape) to help disguise the depth of the box behind the frame.

The sides of the shadowbox are generally less noticeable if they are painted to match the wall on which the box will hang. In some cases, the sides of the box can even be covered with matching wallpaper. If the box is to be placed on a wall paneled in dark wood, the sides of the box can be painted in an almost-black shade of brown to more or less match the hue

Fig. 8–7 You can often save some money by buying shadowbox kits, such as this one by Woodline, rather than preassembled and finished boxes.

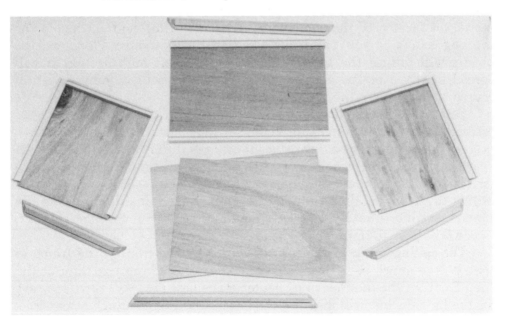

of the wood wall. The use of flat black paint will generally make the sides stand out even more than they would in a bright color.

Lighting

Set designers for the stage or for films have one major advantage over the builder of miniature rooms or shadowboxes: They can position their light *above* the stage. But there is seldom room above a shadowbox for the indirect lighting effects that are used on the stage.

It is also seldom possible to provide perfectly even lighting in a 12-inch-deep box. You will see some ways to provide scale-size ceiling and table lighting in Chapter 4, but that is really effective only in simulating night scenes. For daylight effects, the shadowbox itself must be modified with built-in lighting or with a translucent ceiling.

You could provide a suitable degree of illumination by simply installing one of the picture-frame lights that are intended to accent paintings and portraits. These lights clamp to the picture frame and use tubular screw-in light bulbs of the type used in showcases.

Alternatively, you can install a spotlight in your own ceiling, which is often how museums and art galleries display their collections. However, it is difficult to get enough illumination in the rear corners of the shadowbox with either method. The use of slanted sidewalls and ceilings that are installed for stage sets is described in Chapter 9. This is one of the more effective ways of avoiding dark corners in shadowboxes.

The most effective way to illuminate a shadowbox is to have a translucent plastic ceiling, which will allow natural daytime light to enter from above. Then a small one- or two-tube fluorescent light can be placed on the top of the shadowbox to provide illumination during the evening hours. If you use translucent white or frosted Plexiglas, the plastic will diffuse the light from the fluorescent bulb so that it will spread evenly over the entire ceiling. Scale-size ceiling lamps must, of course, be hung from the plastic ceiling.

Some miniatures shops sell vacuum-formed white plastic ornate-tile ceilings that were common in Victorian (and earlier) homes and businesses. These can serve as translucent ceilings if they are left unpainted.

If several shadowboxes are to be stacked on top of one another to form a bookcase or corner-cupboard arrangement, some type of false ceiling must be installed to hide the fluorescent bulbs illuminating the Plexiglas. Unfortunately, there are no kits that provide for false ceilings, so you will have to improvise.

The ceiling can be angled downward from the front of the frame so that it is as much as 2 inches lower at the rear of the box than at the open front, in the manner of a theater stage set. This will provide space for the lighting but will disguise the lowered ceiling as much as possible.

If the shadowbox is mounted somewhere below the eye level of the viewer, the angled-down ceiling will not be noticeable.

The actual top of the shadowbox can very well be open so that the floor of the shadowbox above it conceals the light bulb and fixture that provide the ceiling illumination. The Plexiglas ceiling can be supported by scale-model corner moldings cemented and perhaps tacked lightly to the walls. With this system, the Plexiglas must be about ¹⁄₈ inch thick to prevent any sagging.

You must leave several 1-inch or larger holes in the sides of the box to provide ventilation for the heat that will build up from the lights. The fixture should be isolated from any wood or flammable plastic with about 6 layers of aluminum foil so that the heat cannot cause a fire. A professional cabinetmaker who specializes in store fixtures and display cases can help you install the lighting fixtures in any of your shadowbox dioramas.

The special-effects illumination through "open" windows, as described in Chapter 10, provides lighting that is almost eerie in its realism. This type of lighting relies on either the natural light from the room, in which case the sides of the box must be exposed to room light, or small incandescent Fluorette bulbs installed behind false interior walls and insulated against any fire hazard.

The effect of such illumination is to duplicate the sunlight that comes through the windows of a full-size room. This type of open-window lighting does not provide the even level of lighting that is possible with illuminated ceilings, but it is very realistic.

The best possible combination of lighting is to incorporate all three forms of diorama lighting: the scale-size table and ceiling lamps, hidden full-ceiling illumination, and open-window illumination. Installing all three allows you to duplicate almost precisely the lighting effects found in real rooms during bright daylight (the ceiling and open-window lights), under hazy sunlight or early morning conditions (the open-window lights), or nighttime illumination (using only the scale-size ceiling and table lamps).

Accessibility

Very few of the kits or ready-built shadowboxes provide for access to the inside of the box after the glass front is in place. Fewer still provide any easy means of replacing a broken glass front. In fact, most of them do not even include the actual glass because it would be so easily broken during shipment. A glass shop or hardware store will cut a piece of glass for the front of almost any size shadowbox for as little as a dollar or two.

It is never a good idea to omit the glass front. If you leave the glass out, you will have to dust off the miniature furniture and bric-a-brac as often as you dust your full-size furnishings. The glass front does not

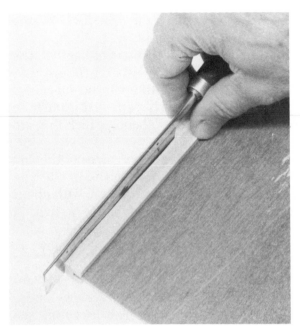

Fig. 8–8 If the shadowbox kit does not provide for a removable top, you will need to cut off the top edge of the rear frame piece *before* assembling the box. This will permit the glass or top to be removed. Removable glass can be provided for in a similar manner.

Fig. 8–9 The modified upper-rear frame piece allows the roof of this Woodline shadowbox to be removed for access to the interior.

completely stop accumulation of dust, but it slows it down to the point where you should have to dust the miniatures only every three or four years.

You must, however, provide some type of access to the interior of the shadowbox for dusting, rearranging the furniture, or adding items to the diorama. There is really only one "best" way to provide access to the inside of a shadowbox, and few, if any, of the commercial boxes or kits provide it. The entire front frame and glass should be hinged on the side so it opens like a door. The frame shop (or you, if you are so inclined) should be able to install a set of hinges and a magnetic catch or some other type of invisible clasp when they make the frame for the shadowbox. The frame shop can also supply the glass, and they can fit the frame so the glass can be replaced easily if it does get broken.

With the side-hinged frame and glass, you will be assured of having access to the inside of the box regardless of whether you mount the box on the wall or stack it in a bookcase. If you are building angled sidewalls or false ceilings, they can be permanently installed by adding a hinged glass front. Otherwise, a wall or ceiling panel would have to be removable to provide access to the interior.

If you are assembling a kit shadowbox to rest on a shelf, you may be able to provide access to the room or the glass by simply sawing off one of the flanges that holds either the glass or the plywood ceiling (see figure 8–8 and 8–9). However, the work must be done before the kit is assembled.

Stagecraft in Miniature

The similarities between the people who design and build theater stage settings and the miniaturist may not be obvious, but we are, in fact, practicing almost the same art. The only major difference between a stage set and a shadowbox diorama is the size: We build our scenes for 6-inch-tall people, while stage designers create for 6-foot-tall people.

Set-Design Basics

The stage set designer is faced with almost the same limitations as is the miniaturist creating a shadowbox diorama. There is a limited amount of depth on the stage because the actors must stay as close to the audience as possible. The miniaturist must limit the depth of any shadowbox to 12 inches or less to make it suitable for hanging on a wall or displaying on a shelf. The wise miniaturist tries to keep the viewing angle about the same as that for a stage set: The floor should be just below the eye level of a person of average height.

The most important lessons the miniaturist can learn from the stage set designer involve the use of forced perspective. It is extremely rare to encounter on the stage the straight-back sidewalls that are common in many shadowbox rooms. The impression of being within a room is conveyed on stage by opening the walls outward, so every member of the audience can see *both* the right and the left wall at the same time. If you follow that rule with your shadowboxes, you will never have to worry about those dark corners at the rear of the shadowbox, because natural light from the open front will fall into the corners.

Those angled walls on stage also serve to provide a forced sense of perspective, so the rooms appear to be deeper than they actually are.

Fig. 9–1 Fred Wilson's 1880-era blacksmith shop diorama. The sidewalls are angled toward the front, like those in a theater stage set. (The back wall is 14 inches long and the glass front wall is 21 inches long.)

That is precisely the effect a miniaturist wants to create in a shadowbox scene. The stage set designer cannot use forced perspective with the furniture or doors (for example, making them smaller at the back of the room to suggest distance) because the actors do not diminish in size just because they step toward the rear of the stage. That means that the stage set designer must plan his or her scenes in almost exactly the same way as the miniaturist, namely for the use of full-size doors and furniture. The set designer's use of color and painted-on shadows can also be most effective in any shadowbox diorama.

Unfortunately, there isn't room in this one book to demonstrate all of the tricks of the masters in stagecraft, but I recommend *Scene Design and Stage Lighting* by W. Oren Parker and Harvey K. Smith (Holt, Rinehart and Winston, 4th ed., 1979) if you want to learn more than I can offer here. The special effects used by the motion picture set designers can also be most helpful in suggesting that there is a more to the scene than what you can see. The use of mirrors and rear-illumination scenes is explained in Chapter 10.

Forced Perspective

The number one rule for a realistic shadowbox diorama is that neither of the two sidewalls should go straight back. Both sidewalls should angle inward toward the center of the box, like those in the blacksmith shop diorama shown in figure 9–1. This is an example of the art of forced perspective because the walls are positioned at the angles we perceive when actually standing inside the room. You might also think of it as a built-in "wide-angle" effect, as if seen through a camera's wide-angle lens.

Yes, you will lose a few square inches of valuable floor space inside the shadowbox, but you can compensate for that by simply making the box bigger in the first place. If, for example, you want the back wall to be 12 inches long, then you will need to start with a showdowbox that is at least 18 inches wide to leave room for the sidewalls to angle inward.

The angled sidewalls serve two purposes: They make the room look about twice as deep as it is, and they allow the light from the front of the shadowbox to reach the rear corners more effectively. The net result is that the room looks much more realistic than it would if the walls went straight back. The viewer is more easily deceived into feeling that he or she really is inside the shadowbox room, and that, of course, is the ultimate aim of the miniaturist's art.

There are several alternatives to the direct frontal view that you obtain when both sidewalls are angled in the same way. You might consider modeling one corner of a room, rather than the entire room as Charles Claudon has done with his "Malkata, 1453 B.C." Egyptian diorama (figure 9–4). There is no "back" wall. Instead, two sidewalls

Fig. 9–2 View through the roof shows the false interior walls and posts assembled to duplicate the rough walls of a real blacksmith shop.

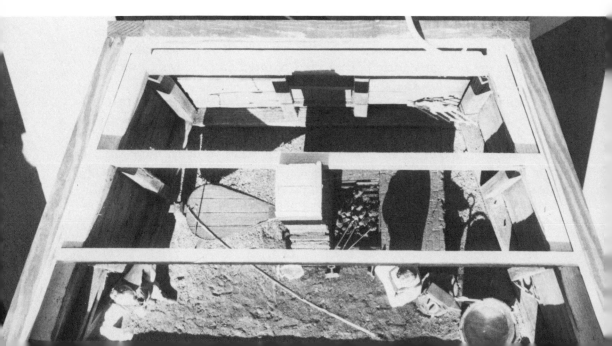

Fig. 9–3 The Wilson Works "stage set" shadowbox is available as an easy-to-assemble kit.

slope toward the rear of the shadowbox from near the forward corners (see figure 9–5). This also has the effect of drawing the viewer's eyes into the room, and it makes it somewhat easier to get even light distribution near the rear of the shadowbox.

Designers of full-size stage sets go to even further extremes to help capture the audience's attention by placing the walls at about every imaginable angle, *except* 90 degrees. Charles Claudon's "April, 1912" diorama (figures 9–6 and 9–7) and his "Soldier's Home, 1943" (shown in the color section) are fine examples of the use of a number of short wall sections set at a variety of angles. Somehow, the technique also helps to imply that there is a whole lot more house on the other side of some of those walls.

Betty Dick's Colonial-style entryway and staircase scene is a masterpiece in implying the existence of a complete house from a single room (figure 9–8). She gives hints of other rooms through open doorways, and those stairs certainly do lead somewhere.

Fig. 9–4 Charles Claudon's "Malkata, 1453 B.C.," uses the angled walls and indirect lighting techniques developed for theater stage sets. *Photo by Charles Claudon.*

A Model of a Miniature

The best way to create the effects achieved by stage set designers is to follow their lead and make a paper model or a mock-up of the scene. A stage set designer generally starts with a two-dimensional sketch of the audience's view of the scene, followed by an overhead or "plan" view. These drawings are then used to create paper or cardboard walls and furniture to double-check the effect in three dimensions.

You would be wise to follow the same sequence, but you can take a giant shortcut to the finished product by making the mock-up walls from thick paper or corrugated cardboard and fitting them inside your shadowbox. The cardboard walls can then served as full-size patterns for the plywood or foam-core walls.

If you have the miniature furniture, doors, and windows for the scene, you can even position them where they should be in the mock-up scene. The doors and windows can simply be taped to the walls temporarily to check their effect. It is much easier to relocate a door or window that way, or to cut a shorter or longer cardboard wall, than it is to do your adjusting with the plywood or foam-core walls. You will be far more likely to get precisely the effect you want, too, when you take the time to cut, fit, and refit the walls until the angles are perfect for the scene.

Fred Wilson's 1880-Era Blacksmith Shop

The walls of Fred Wilson's blacksmith shop diorama are placed directly on the walls of the shadowbox. The shadowbox itself is a kit designed and sold by Fred. (It is shown in figure 9–3.) The shadowbox could be every bit as effective if it housed a Victorian sitting room, a colonial bedroom, or any one of the other conventional dollhouse miniatures scenes.

Fred wanted to try his hand at creating a somewhat more unusual scene. The walls and ceiling are individual wood planks and beams that he cut from standard-size lumber, but Northeastern or Midwest dollhouse wood could be used as well. The handmade forge is cast in plaster, with the brick carved by hand. The anvil, too, is hand-carved from a block of plaster. The wood bucket on the floor is filled with epoxy casting resin to simulate the water used to cool the just-forged iron. The floor is covered with scale-size sawdust. The shovels, horseshoes, and other small details are all lead and tin castings from Metal Miniatures.

Fig. 9–5 Plan of Charles Claudon's "Malkata, 1453 B.C.," shadowbox diorama.

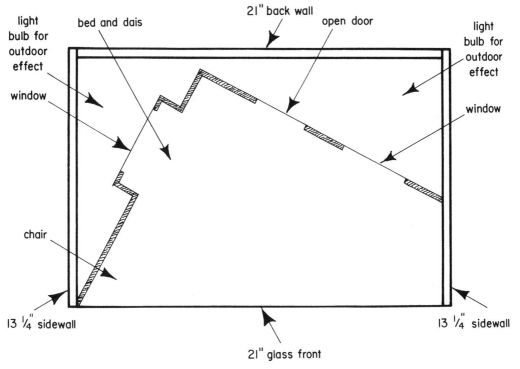

Fig. 9–6 Outdoor lights and an indirect light beneath a translucent panel supplement the table lamp in Charles Claudon's "April, 1912" shadowbox diorama. *Photo by Charles Claudon.*

Charles Claudon's Malkata, 1453 B.C.

Charles Claudon makes just about everything for his rooms by hand. His scenes could be re-created by using commercial windows, doors, and furnishings, and they are near enough to the size of ready-built shadowboxes that purchased shadowboxes could be used to re-create similar scenes.

"Malkata, 1453 B.C." is his idea of what Pharaoh Tutankhamun's bedroom might have looked like. The walls of the Pharaoh's room were probably made of mud bricks covered with a stucco of rough lime. The floor was probably trampled earth. Charles used textured paints and real dirt to try to duplicate these textures. The walls of the room are placed well forward of the walls of the shadowbox to allow the use of incandescent bulbs in the corners, which simulate sunlight streaming through the high windows.

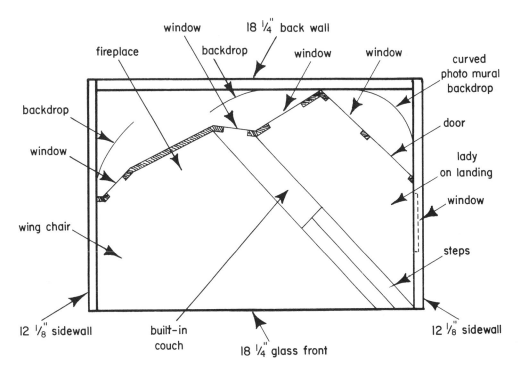

Fig. 9–7 Charles Claudon's "April, 1912" shadowbox diorama.

Fig. 9–8 All of the woodwork and furniture in Betty Dick's "Colonial Entryway" is made from commercial wood or easy-to-assemble kits. *Courtesy Betty Dick.*

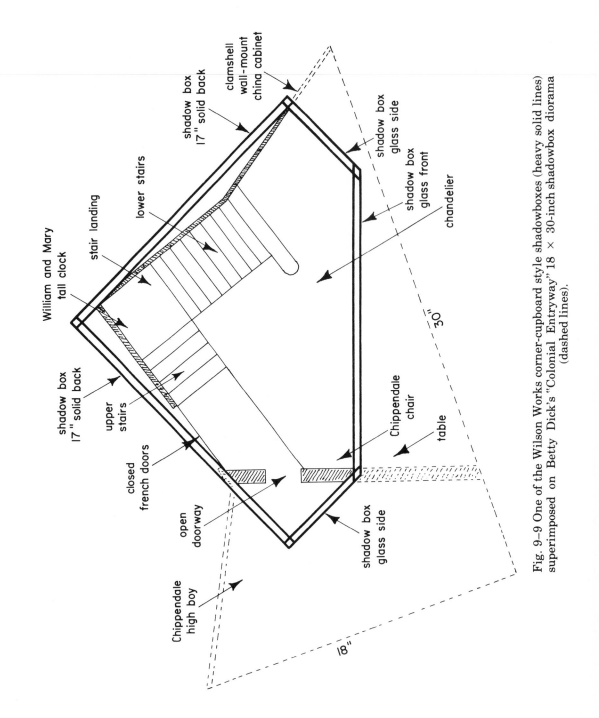

clamshell
wall-mount
china cabinet

shadow box
17" solid back

shadow box
glass side

shadow box
glass front

chandelier

lower stairs

stair landing

William and Mary
tall clock

30"

shadow box
17" solid back

upper
stairs

closed
french doors

open
doorway

Chippendale
chair

table

shadow box
glass side

Chippendale
high boy

18"

Fig. 9–9 One of the Wilson Works corner-cupboard style shadowboxes (heavy solid lines) superimposed on Betty Dick's "Colonial Entryway" 18 × 30-inch shadowbox diorama (dashed lines).

Charles Claudon's April, 1912

The sunken living room of Charles Claudon's "April, 1912" diorama adds a dimension that is usually not found in shadowbox dioramas. There isn't a 90° wall angle in the scene, although a short portion of both the right and left walls does lead straight back toward the rear wall of the shadowbox.

As usual, Charles handcrafted the furniture, and he handpainted a Masterpiece Museum Miniatures "Victorian housewife" to add a touch of life to the scene. The lamp was crafted from strip metal by L. Kummerow. Photo murals from calendar art and magazines are illuminated with bare light bulbs to simulate the outdoor scenes behind the windows.

Betty Dick's Colonial Entryway

Betty Dick assembled her "Colonial Entryway" entirely from commercial parts and kits. The staircase and banister were fitted together from Northeastern milled wood. Midwest mahogany was used for the treads.

The scene is just one side of a square cabinet Betty is completing, which will have a different room on each side. The entryway and the room adjacent to it occupy and area about 18×30 inches, but the entryway alone can easily be fitted into a corner-cupboard style shadowbox, like the one Fred Wilson produces in kit form. Figure 9–9 shows the walls of Betty's room that extend beyond the Wilson Works corner cupboard shadowbox.

The corner-cupboard types of shadowboxes obviously lend themselves nicely to the use of stage set designs that depict a single corner of the room. You can increase the realism of the scene by angling the walls in a manner similar to that used in Betty's diorama.

10

Special Effects

Artists who create the indoor and outdoor scenes for television and films have developed stagecraft to its ultimate form. These artists, like set designers for the theater, have much in common with the miniaturist because they often must "miniaturize" scenes from real life. The special effects people at the film studios have developed a number of tricks that will work equally well in a scale of one inch to the foot. The scenes you see on television or in a movie theater are defined and limited by the edges of the screen. You have that same control over the viewers of a shadowbox diorama, but the scene is defined and limited by the edges of the frame around the shadowbox.

The most important lessons the special effects people have to offer us miniaturists are those that make the scenes seem to be true to life by suggesting that there is more to the scene than meets the eye. Sometimes those suggestions take the form of visual tricks. Obviously miniaturists will never have to simulate explosions or flights into space, but there are some special-effects tricks that can lend incredible realism to almost any shadowbox diorama.

Actors for Miniature Sets

Miniaturist hobbyists are rather strongly divided on the subject of whether or not to include people in their dollhouses and shadowbox dioramas. Some miniaturists would rather leave the rooms empty so they can imagine themselves and their relatives in the rooms. Others, who do not want to stray from the dollhouse theme, prefer to populate their miniature rooms with toy dolls. The third school feels that lifelike

Fig. 10–1 Realistic miniature figures can often bring a scene such as this to life, as seen in the next photo.

figures merely extend the realism of the scene, enhancing the furniture and other miniatures in the room.

Some miniaturists prefer to use dolls that look more like toy dolls than miniatures of real people in their dollhouses or dioramas. This is one of the countless areas of the miniatures hobby where you can do exactly what pleases you and produce a work of art that is unique unto itself. The only limitation is that you should keep any dolls that are to represent adults in the 5- to 6½-inch range in order to match the scale of the furniture. Dolls that represent children can of course be smaller in proportion.

I have tried to illustrate only realistic dolls in the dioramas in order to give you some idea of just how lifelike such characters can appear in a miniature scene. A realistic replica of a ¹⁄₁₂-scale person can be very effective in a shadowbox diorama. Probably figures should not appear in every room scene, because some rooms will have more impact on the viewer without the presence of "people." You will see examples in this

Fig. 10–2 Cecil Boyd Austin painted the blacksmith and Pat Milhollin painted the kibitzer that enliven this diorama.

Fig. 10–3 The blacksmith (right) is available ready to paint from Masterpiece Museum Miniatures. Other figures are sold by ceramic crafts shops.

Fig. 10–4 These cast figurines, made by Master Museum Miniatures and painted by Cecil Boyd Austin, add a touch of life to this Victorian shadowbox diorama.

chapter and in Chapter 9 that may help you decide whether or not to include actors in your miniature "sets."

Most of the figures illustrated here are made by Masterpiece Museum Miniatures. Cecil Boyd Austin applied her artistic touch to the grandfather and daughter shown in figure 1–15 and the blacksmith in figure 10–2, Pat Milhollin painted the kibitzer in the same scene, and Charles Claudon painted the Victorian-era mother in figure 9–6. There are several dozen different ready-to-paint figures available from most miniatures shops. You may find additional figures at a ceramic crafts shop. The ceramic shop can also provide some help in painting the figures or perhaps even have them painted for you.

Hobby shops that carry military miniatures also have books and paints for scale-model people, and they may even be able to paint the figures for you. The realism of the paint job will generally have a direct relationship to the amount of time spent on the figure. For do-it-yourselfers, the book *Military Miniatures* by Simon Goodenough (Chilton, 1978) has excellent instructions for converting and painting these scale-size figures.

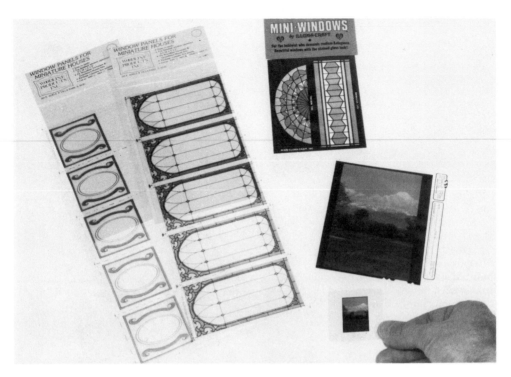

Fig. 10–5 Miniature shops sell a wide variety of printed plastic replicas of stained glass. Camera shops can **make** 4 × 5 color transparencies (lower right) from any 35mm or larger color slide.

Fig. 10–6 Two of Cir-Kit's 12-volt Fluorette bulbs can provide enough light for the rear-projection effects with a 4 × 5 transparency (right). The plastic stained-glass panel was used to make up the difference in the height of the window and the transparency.

Fig. 10–7 The use of a color transparency, illuminated from the rear, gives a three-dimensional effect that is not apparent here.

There are several brands of dolls that fall somewhere between the toy and the sculpted replicas illustrated here. The British-made Peggy Nisbet collector's dolls are suitable for any dollhouse or diorama in 1/12 scale. These dolls have clothing made of real cloth and they usually represent historical figures, including queens, kings, American presidents, and Williamsburg colonial-era people. Adults and teenagers are included in the series. There are also several different series of similar-size dolls that are imported from Hong Kong, Taiwan, and Korea for sale in toy stores.

If you consider the miniatures hobby to be a three-dimensional art form (as I do), then the re-creation of true-to-life people to inhabit the

Fig. 10–8 The triangular spaces behind the interior walls of shadowbox dioramas can be used to hide the light bulbs that provide rear-projection illumination for color transparencies in "open" windows.

true-to-life rooms can only emphasize the artistic aspect of the hobby. In the world of miniatures, the presence of realistic people in the scene is definitely a "special effect" that goes one step beyond the re-creation of the furniture and accessories.

Rear-Projection Window Scenes

One of the standard types of special effects used on television and in films is the use of a second film that is projected onto a plastic screen behind the actors to make them appear to be outside the studio, riding along on a horse, for example, or driving in an automobile. Films of the countryside moving along behind the horse or the automobile are projected onto the plastic screen from behind. Rear projection is being replaced by more effective techniques for films, but it will work quite nicely for the miniaturist.

The only place where a miniaturist needs to use scenes of the outside world is behind the windows of a dollhouse or diorama. It is

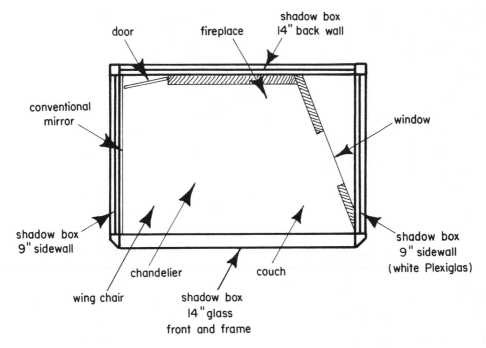

Fig. 10-9 Plan of the Victorian sitting-room shadowbox diorama.

Fig. 10-10 A glass shop can cut a mirror to fit against one of the end walls in a shadowbox of any size.

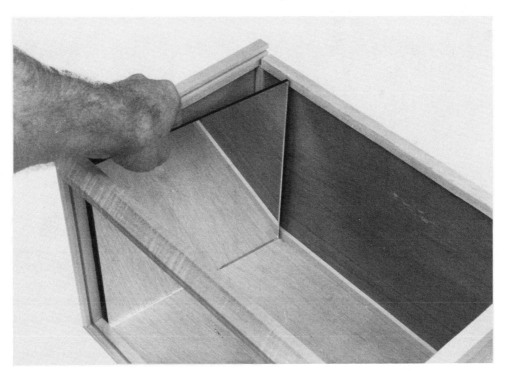

Fig. 10–11 The mirror on the wall of the Victorian sitting-room diorama seems to double the size of the scene.

Fig. 10–12 Eve Endlich's garden scene is repeated infinitely by the mirrors on the two sides of the shadowbox.

incredibly simple to apply the technique of rear projection to make the view from a miniature window look exactly like a view into the real world.

The old method of depicting outdoor scenes was to place a color photograph taken from a calendar or magazine on a wall a few inches behind the dollhouse or diorama windows. A light bulb was placed near the "outside" dollhouse wall so that it would shine on the photograph. This effect is better than no scene at all, but it looks exactly like what it is: a photograph that is being illuminated with a light bulb. The scene does not glow with the light of reality—the light bulb does. With the rear-projection technique, the scene itself "lives" with a glow that is almost precisely like that of the real world.

You can get an idea of the realism of rear projection by comparing a color slide with a print of the same scene. The print lacks the three-dimensional effect of the slide and is less realistic. Unfortunately, we can duplicate only some of the realism in the two-dimensional illustrations here, but visit a camera shop and compare the difference between slides and prints for yourself.

Ask at your local camera shop how much it would cost to make 4 × 5-inch or 5 × 8-inch blowups of slides. The 4 × 5 enlargement should cost between $15 and $20, and a 5 × 8 enlargement may run two or three times that amount. Be specific and let the person know that you want a *transparency,* not a print. Almost any camera shop can order an enlargement of a slide that was taken with almost any size camera.

You can even take a photograph of your own backyard and use it with the rear-projection technique in the windows of your dollhouse or diorama. That 4 × 5-inch or 5 × 8-inch slide or transparency can be taped to the outside of the window in your diorama or dollhouse and a source of light provided from the "outside" to illuminate the transparency. The amount of outside light you will need will depend upon the brightness of the inside of the diorama. There should be more light coming through the window than exists in the room for a daylight scene.

Fig. 10–13 Norm Nielsen's "infinity" shadowbox has a two-way mirror for the front panel that partially reflects the patterns of the outside world.

Fig. 10–14 With the exterior room lights off, the infinity box repeats the scene inside again and again to simulate an endless hallway.

If you are using a color transparency of a moonlight scene, then the interior lights should be brighter than the transparency. You will also have to place a sheet of translucent white Plexiglas or another form of plastic between the light source and the transparency to diffuse the light so that there will be no "hot spots" from the light bulb.

In effect, you will be doing just what the special-effects departments of film studios do to provide rear-projection realism, except that the "film" for your scene is also the screen. Your miniature should also be much less expensive than those used by the studios. A single 4 × 5 transparency can be cut into two 2 × 5-inch scenes for use behind two windows.

The Victorian sitting room in this chapter (and figures 1–15 and 8–6) has a single window with a color transparency providing rear-projection realism. The outside wall of the shadowbox itself (behind the interior wall with the window and transparency) is white translucent Plexiglas. This shadowbox has been mounted on a wall where natural light provides the illumination for the rear projection during the day and a nearby table lamp provides the illumination at night.

A light bulb could also have been placed inside the shadowbox in the empty triangle of space between the sitting room's wall and the outside wall of the shadowbox. White Plexiglas would then have to be placed between the light bulb and the color transparency to diffuse the light. The top of the triangular area would also have to be open so that the heat from the light bulb could escape, and the wood and cardboard walls would have to be insulated with aluminum foil so they would not catch fire from the heat of the light bulb.

It would be far better to build the shadowbox 3 or 4 inches deeper than the room (like Charles Claudon's dioramas in Chapter 9), so there would be room for a small fluorescent light fixture inside the box. A single fixture could provide enough light for a half-dozen windows with color transparencies behind them. This would also allow you to place windows on the rear wall of the diorama as well as on the sidewalls. The top of the shadowbox would have to be cut away to ventilate the heat from the fluorescent fixture.

It's All Done with Mirrors

The phrase "It's all done with mirrors" has been used to describe all sorts of magical effects. In some instances, the phrase is a perfect description of what you are seeing. Many of the seemingly bottomless pits or shafts that are seen in fantasy and science-fiction films are created with several mirrors. The mirrors can be used almost as effecitvely with shadowbox dioramas to double the apparent size of the scene or to provide the "infinity" effect for special display shadowbox scenes.

The mirror on the left wall of the Victorian sitting room (figure 10–11) doubles the size of the room from most viewing angles, and it also helps to amplify the light coming through the rear-projection scene in the window on the opposite wall. Eve Endlich used mirrors on three walls of her garden diorama (figure 10–12). If you look into either side of the box, the garden scene seems to extend into infinity.

Norm Nielsen's "infinity box" Christmas diorama (figures 10–13 and 10–14) uses a two-way mirror on the front side and a one-way mirror on the back wall to produce an almost infinite number of repititions of the scene inside the box. Any one of these three tricks might produce the effect you want for your shadowbox diorama.

The Invisible Mirror

The mirrors used in the Victorian sitting room and garden scenes are conventional mirrors, and you can see the $1/8$-inch-thick black line that appears at the edges of the mirrors. That line is the only telltale sign that a mirror is being used, however, and it is possible to avoid it.

Almost any glass shop can order ¼-inch-thick two-way mirror glass. The two-way mirror is produced in the same way as a conventional mirror, except the dark green paint that protects the reflective surface is *not* applied. This leaves the reflective surface visible from either side of the glass. If you place the reflective side toward the interior of your diorama, there will be only the slightest hairline indication that the mirror is there. Unfortunately, the unprotected reflective surface scratches very easily, so you must clean it carefully and gently.

The Infinity Box

The "infinity box" is simply a shadowbox with a conventional mirror on the rear wall and a two-way mirror on the front wall. The illumination for the scene inside the shadowbox must come from lights placed inside the shadowbox between the two mirrors. When the light inside the box is greater than the light outside it, you can see through the two-way mirror on the front.

Fig. 10–15 The interior of the infinity box seen from the back with the conventional one-way mirror removed. The sidewalls of the inner box are translucent white Plexiglas. The upside-down camera is reflected in the two-way glass on the front of the box.

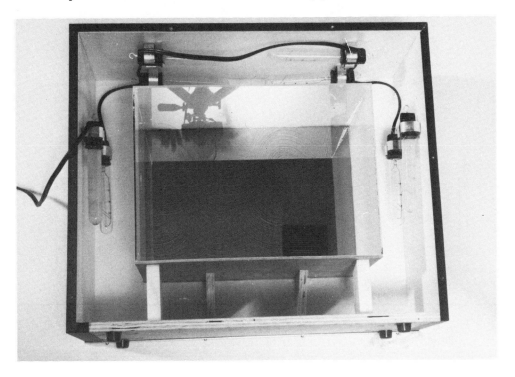

The mirror, however, still reflects the scene inside, and that reflection is bounced back and forth between the conventional mirror on the back wall and the two-way mirror on the front. The reflection repeats the scene into what appears to be an ever-darkening infinity. If the lights inside the box are turned off, the two-way mirror appears to be nothing more than a common mirror.

Figure 10–16 identifies the parts that make up the infinity box. The drawing shows the box as it would appear if you were looking down directly through the top of the box with the lid and ceiling removed. The clear glass panel on the front of the box (A) merely protects the box and gives it the appearance of a framed painting.

The *secret* to the infinity box is the two-way mirror panel (C). Two-way mirrors are expensive, so this panel is kept as small as possible and supported on all four edges by an opaque plastic panel (B). Panel B simply holds the two-way mirror (C) in the center of the box and blocks any light from inside the box from glowing through the front of the box.

A two-way mirror is often seen in spy movies or police interrogation rooms, where one surface looks like an ordinary mirror, but the opposite

Fig. 10–16 Norm Nielsen's "infinity" shadowbox viewed in cross section from the top of the box.

A $17^3/_4 \times 21^1/_2''$ clear glass front
B $17^3/_4 \times 21^1/_2''$ plastic frame with $10^3/_4 \times 14^1/_4''$ hole to hold the two-way mirror
C $10^3/_4 \times 14^1/_4''$ two-way mirror (mirror faces back wall)
D $1/_4''$ plywood and $1/_4''$ white Plexiglas floor

E $3/_4''$ plywood sides, top, and bottom
F Lights for sides
G $1/_4''$ white Plexiglas sides and top
H $10^3/_4 \times 14^1/_4''$ conventional mirror
I Lights above inner box
J $1 \times 2''$ wood supports for floor
K $1/_4''$ thick plastic back wall, $17^3/_4 \times 21^3/_4''$

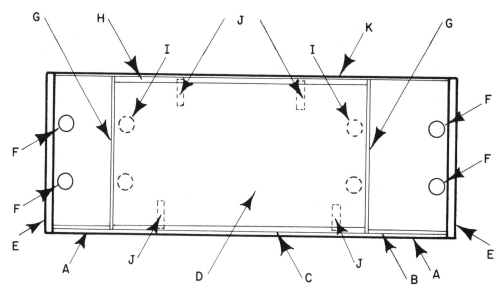

surface acts as see-through glass. This two-way mirror is mounted in the shadowbox so the mirror side faces toward the rear wall (H), which is a conventional one-way mirror.

The two-way mirror (C) will function as a see-through glass *only* if the light on the mirrored side (inside the box, in this case) is brighter than the light on the outside. This is why built-in light bulbs are placed on both sides and on the top of the Infinity Box. When these built-in lights are off, the front of the box looks like a solid piece of dark gray tinted glass (Figure 10–13). When the lights are turned on, the two-way mirror repeats (or reflects) the scene inside the box, and it repeats (or reflects) whatever is in the conventional mirror (H) at the back of the box. The scene is reflected and repeated almost to infinity (see figures 10–14 and 10–15).

The sides and top (G) of the box-within-a-box are white Plexiglas, which allows the light from the bulbs on the tops and sides to reach the scene. The scene sits on another piece of white Plexiglas, which is backed with plywood so no light passes through it. The plastic frame (B) that supports the two-way mirror, as well as the outer sides, top, bottom, and back wall of the infinity box are also made of materials that will not transmit light.

Only the scene inside the box is illuminated so that the images of the scene will bounce back and forth from mirrors C and H. You can see the scene and its reflections only because the front mirror is two-way.

The infinity effect is incredibly realistic once you achieve a balance between the inside light and the outside light so that the images inside the box are bright. If there is too much outside light, the images repeat only a few times before vanishing into darkness. The effect is startling because the bright inside lights allow you to look right into the box without seeing your own image. All you see are the multiple reflections of whatever is inside the box stretching back into what appears to be an endless hallway.

DOLLHOUSES

11

Quick-Build Kits and Systems

The miniaturist no longer has to build a dollhouse from scratch from gigantic sheets of plywood. Today, every style and size dollhouse imaginable is available either as a kit or as $^1/_{12}$-scale plans. There are at least four different systems of dollhouse construction that use easy-to-cut components, so you can custom-build a dollhouse with only a little more effort than that required to assemble a kit.

The fundamental difference between the kits and the systems is that the kits require almost no cutting or sawing. The systems all require you to cut parts to fit, but the parts themselves are designed to be cut very easily with just hand tools. Because the wall panels in most of the systems are only a few inches high, you can cut the window and door openings in upper and lower "halves," so only straight cuts are needed. The wood used is relatively soft, so a razor saw, a picture-frame cutting saw, or a tool such as the "chopper" shown in figure 11–17 can be used to provide nearly splinter-free cuts with only a light amount of pressure. The systems take the work out of custom-building a dollhouse but leave you the pleasure of creating something with your own hands.

The dollhouse kits allow you to bypass all the measuring, fitting, and cutting, but you can still be creative by "renovating" the kits with more realistic windows, doors, and trim. The appearance of the kits can be completely altered with new windows and doors and by modifications to the pitch of the roof, described in Chapter 6. You can, indeed, custom-build a home in miniature using the simplified systems or the kits that take the work out of the hobby but leave the fun.

Fig. 11–1 The parts in most of the dollhouse kits are completely precut, so only light sanding, assembly, and painting is required. This is S/W Crafts' Grandpa's House kit. *Courtesy S/W Crafts, Inc.*

The Woodline System

The systems of dollhouse construction used by Woodline and by Our House are very similar, but they differ in detail. The Woodline system has milled-wood corner posts that hold the walls in position. The walls themselves are made from 2½-inch-high wood panels that have a smooth interior and a shiplap or clapboard-style exterior.

About four panels are needed to make a single-story wall. The vertical portions of the window and door frames are U-shaped wood pieces that hold the 2½-inch wall panels in position at the edges of the windows and doors. The Woodline kits provide precut pieces of all of the wall panels.

If you want to custom-build a dollhouse with Woodline's system, you simply cut the panels to fill in the wall areas between the windows in the same manner that Woodline does in the kits, and glue the components together with white glue. Two of their 2½-inch panels are equal to the more or less standard 5-inch window height.

The only disadvantage to the system is that the vertical corner moldings are visible inside the house. However, you can hide them by filling in the walls with ¹⁄₁₆-inch cardboard or Northeastern wood sheets to provide simple square corners. You must install the extra interior wall panels on either the Woodline kits or in a house made with the Woodline system if you are particular about the inside corners of the rooms.

The Woodline windows, like those in most dollhouse kits, are simplified versions of the real thing. The better-detailed working windows from firms such as Carlson Miniatures, Houseworks, and Maxwell House can be fitted if you modify some of the window openings during the construction stages. The Woodline vertical window-frame channels will not be needed if you use these accessory windows.

The Our House System

The Our House kits and system of custom-building from components uses 1¾-inch-high wall strips milled with shiplap or clapboard detail on

Fig. 11–2 Use a combination square when assembling any dollhouse. Woodline's slotted corner posts and vertical window-frame channels hold the clapboard wall pieces in alignment.

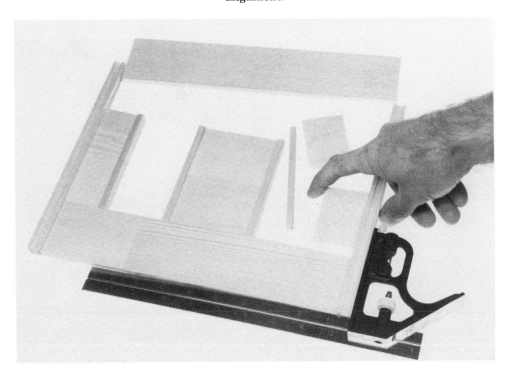

Fig. 11–3 The Woodline system uses the corner posts as built-in assembly jigs. Use white glue when assembling the system's components.

Fig. 11–4 Woodline kits include a spacer jig to position the horizontal mullion strip. Windows in most kits are very simplified in order to keep costs down.

the outside and a smooth surface on the inside. There is a tongue on the top of each panel and a groove on the bottom. The tongue-and-groove arrangement helps to make each wall more rigid than they would be if the panels were simply butted together.

The corner joints in the Our House system are conventional overlapping joints like those on the corners of a wood fruit box. A milled-wood angle hides the corner joints and provides realistic corner trim. The inside corners are clean and smooth like those of a finished full-size house.

Narrower sidewall strips allow the sidewalls to be built to a peak of almost any height in increments of either $5/8$ or $1^3/4$ inch. Special beveled strips are used under the eaves at the top of sidewalls. L-shape moldings are used to finish the bottom edges of the walls and to support them on

Fig. 11–5 This Victorian mansion was assembled with the foam-core Mini-Boards and vacuum-formed plastic exterior panels from the Handley House system of dollhouse construction. *Courtesy Handley House.*

the foundation blocks. Most of the Our House kits are designed to accept Houseworks windows without any extra cutting.

The Handley House System

The Handley House system of dollhouse construction uses construction methods similar to those used for plywood dollhouse shells, except that the plywood is replaced with the far lighter Handley House Mini-Board $1/12$-inch-thick foam-core board. The board is specially treated with a plastic coating. The Mini-Board is then covered with a variety of vacuum-molded plastic panels to simulate bricks, shiplap siding, shingles, tiles, or stone. The primary advantage of the system is that it provides scale-thickness walls without the weight of plywood. The foam-core Mini-Board is also much easier to cut than plywood.

Cut lightly through the foam-core board on both sides, then push the board down firmly over the edge of a table or 2×4. The board will break cleanly along the cuts. To cut windows in the foam core, use the diagonal X-cut technique illustrated in figures 2–7 and 2–8 in Chapter 2, or use an electric saber saw with a knife-edge blade.

The Carlson System

The Carlson system of dollhouse construction is available in either precut kits to build specific dollhouses or as bulk stock to be used to custom-build a house. The construction is similar to that used in building a full-size home, except that much fewer framework pieces are required, and the exterior and interior panels are applied in $1^{3}/8$-inch-wide strips.

The exterior molding is milled to duplicate the appearance of shiplap or clapboard siding, and the corners and bases of the walls are trimmed with scale-size boards. The walls are all designed to accept Carlson's preassembled and detailed working windows and doors.

The Northeastern System

Northeastern does not, at present, offer its dollhouse construction system in any precut kits. It does, however, have one of the largest selections of milled-wood angles, moldings, and panels. The Northeastern construction system is very similar to that used to build a full-size house except for the use of fewer and larger framework pieces.

Northeastern's $1/16$-inch-thick sheetwood panels are $3^{1}/2$ inches high, but it also offers a choice of clapboard (shiplap), board and batten, novelty, corrugated, scribed surfaces, milled imitation concrete, corrugated iron, brick, cinder block, and flagstone surfaces. Northeastern also has all the milled-wood moldings needed to make custom-fitted windows and doors as described in Chapter 2.

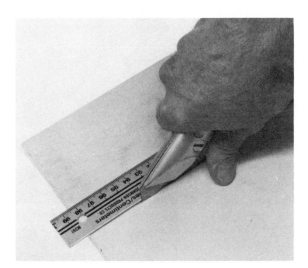

Fig. 11–6 The plastic-coated foam-core Mini-Board, from Handley House, can be cut by making several light slices through the board on both sides of the rigid foam core.

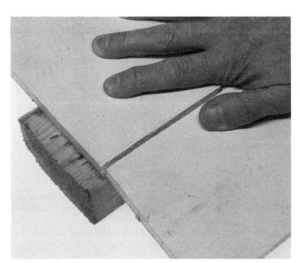

Fig. 11–7 Hold the foam-core board over the edge of a table or a 2×4 and push down firmly on the cuts. The foam-core board will break cleanly along the cuts, even if the cuts were not made all the way through the cardboard surfaces. This slice-and-break technique can be used for cutting styrene or Plexiglas sheets.

Fig. 11–8 Windows can be cut in the foam core using the diagonal method described in Chapter 2 or with an electric saber saw, using a knife-edge blade in the saw.

Fig. 11–9 The Carlson system of dollhouse construction uses a simplified replica of the framing in a real house with wide siding strips and Carlson's preassembled windows and doors. *Courtesy Carlson's Miniatures, Inc.*

The Midwest System

Midwest Products produces a variety of milled-wood sheets, strips, and moldings for miniature dollhouses and dioramas. Its particular system of dollhouse construction consists of simply milled-wood wall panels that stack on edge with interlocking surfaces. Wood angles form the exterior corners to double as both supports for the wall panels and vertical exterior trim.

The Midwest system, like most of the other brands, lends itself nicely to constructing dollhouses to match modified plans of full-size houses.

The Plywood Shell System

Almost any miniatures shop stocks or will order assembled, unfinished plywood dollhouse shells that you can finish and detail to your heart's content. It is possible to get a custom-built shell if you can find a carpenter who will make the house to your specifications. That can often be arranged through the firm that builds the plywood shells for your local miniatures shop.

But a custom-built dollhouse, even if it is just an unfinished shell, can be extremely costly. If, for example, a two-story "in-stock" shell sells for $75, you may find that one of identical size but built to your own design would run about $750.

You may be able to design the house of your dreams around the wall patterns used for the in-stock shells and save most of the custom-cutting expenses. Most of the dollhouse shells are cut with special jigs or

Fig. 11–10 Carlson offers its system in a series of complete dollhouse kits that includes this Sunnywood Farm miniature. *Courtesy Carlson's Miniatures, Inc.*

Fig. 11–11 The shutters, railings, columns, ornate trim, windows, and doors are all included in Carlson's Southern Plantation dollhouse kit. *Courtesy Carlson's Miniatures.*

patterns that are difficult to modify without resorting to a completely hand-cut custom dollhouse, which of course is expensive.

Building from Plans

It is far more difficult than you might imagine to build a dollhouse from plans. Although the plans look almost like cut-out paper walls, they are deceiving. It takes a considerable amount of effort just to collect all the materials, even if you are using one of the various types of dollhouse systems.

Most of us dream of converting some house plan or photograph we have saved into a complete dollhouse. That can be virtually impossible without an incredible number of compromises. For one thing, real houses are meant to be accessible from the inside, while dollhouses must be accessible from the outside.

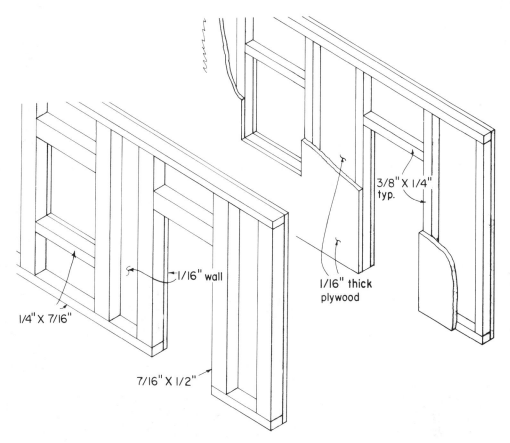

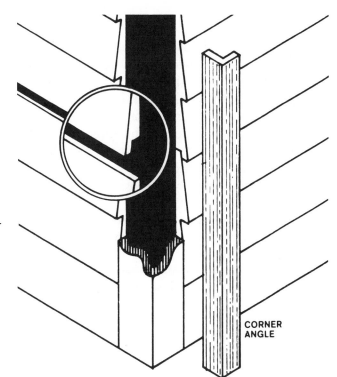

Fig. 11–12 The Northeastern system of dollhouse construction allows you to build ½-inch-thick walls with either two finished sides (right) or with one side open (left). Northeastern offers a wide choice of ¹⁄₁₆-inch-thick exterior panels. *Courtesy Northeastern Scale Models, Inc.*

Fig. 11–13 The Midwest system of dollhouse construction uses interlocking milled-wood wall panels with wood angles at each corner. *Courtesy Midwest Products.*

Fig. 11–14 Batrie Dollhouses offers a modular system of dollhouse kits that allows the builder to begin with a simple core structure, such as shown here, and add a variety of wings and details. *Courtesy Batrie Dollhouses.*

If your dream house is much larger than a one-room cabin, you will have to completely redesign those plans to place all of the rooms on a single plane, the way they are in most dollhouses. It is possible to make a dollhouse with three planes that hinge together, such as J. B. Lundquist's Victorian mansion in Chapter 1 (figure 1–5). But you had better be an experienced cabinetmaker, a proficient modeler or both before you even think about such a complex project and such an expensive one in materials alone.

There are some compromise measures you can take between a simple cabin and a swing-away three-plane, three-story mansion. Many of the firms that sell dollhouse construction systems also offer plans that can be used with their systems to create unique dollhouses.

Before you start working from one of these sets of plans, though, insist that your dealer check with the manufacturer or distributor to be certain that the plans have not already been converted into a precut kit.

If you are working with one of the systems, there is very little saving in cutting your material when it may be available precut.

Most miniatures shops also sell dozens of scale plans to build dollhouses. Generally, these plans are designed for the construction of the dollhouse from sheets of ¹/₂-inch plywood. You may be able to turn them over to a carpenter to have a custom-made house for two or three times the price of a ready-built shell. The first carpenter to contact, of course, is the person who makes the shells for the dealer. If you use these plans, you will have bypassed the difficult process of adapting a real house to the needs of a dollhouse.

Another alternative worth considering is to adapt two or more kits of the same brand to build your dream house. Here you have the advantage of both a plan that works and precut parts. There are suggestions in Chapter 6 on the easy ways to alter the style of a dollhouse by simple changes in the roof.

You may be able to combine the style and shape of a real house with the parts from two or more kits to create a truly unique miniature with a minimum amount of cost. Information and plans on modern homes are available in dozens of magazines available at any large newsstand. The public library should have books of home plans and photographs dating back to the early part of the century.

If you prefer Victorian or Edwardian styles, consider the three books of plans from The American Life Foundation & Study Institute (Figure 11–

Fig. 11–15 This fully detailed exterior, based on the simple structure shown in figure 11–14, looks just like an historical New England colonial mansion. *Courtesy Batrie Dollhouses.*

Fig. 11–16 Dremel's 4-inch table saw for modelers can make quick work of framing a dollhouse with scale-size wood or to cut the parts for custom-built dollhouses with various wood-building "systems" *Courtesy Dremel Manufacturing Co.*

Fig. 11–17 The NorthWest Short Line "Chopper" is a guillotinelike tool that uses a replaceable single-edge razor blade. The tool makes it easy to cut dozens of equal-length framing parts.

Fig. 11–18 Northeastern and Midwest both offer thin sheetwood wall panels. If you cover the cut line with masking tape, scissors can be used to make splinter-free cuts.

Fig. 11–19 Reprints of architectural history books, such as these three from The American Life Foundation, can supply plans and detail drawings if you want to custom-build dollhouse miniatures.

19, check with your bookseller or local library). The books are reprints of actual exterior and interior plans of all sizes of homes and several businesses of the turn-of-the-century era with detail close-ups of doors, windows, and trim.

Similar volumes are available on Colonial, Early American, and virtually any twentieth-century style under the Architecture sections in public libraries and new and used bookstores.

12

Dollhouse Renovation

There may be a way for you to have the dollhouse of your dreams without resorting to building your own or going to the expense of having one custom-built. The biggest bargains in dollhouses are the dollhouse kits made by several manufacturers that are intended specifically for adults. These kits generally have $1/4$- to $1/2$-inch-thick walls and the details and proportions a miniaturist expects from a dollhouse.

The kit and ready-built dollhouses intended for children are often made from $1/8$-inch plywood or even cardboard, and that makes them extremely difficult to renovate to the standards of a custom or handmade dollhouse. Most of the kits, though, can be renovated so that they look every bit as attractive as the best custom-made dollhouse you can buy. And when you do the work yourself, you not only save the expense of someone else's labor, but you have the satisfaction of knowing that your dollhouse is truly a unique, handcrafted original. The lessons and examples in almost every chapter of this book can be applied to any of the adult dollhouse kits to make them into perfect miniature homes.

If you start with a kit, there will be very little cutting and fitting, so the work will progress quite rapidly. But be sure to plan all of the renovations you intend to make to the kit *before* you actually begin to glue or nail it together. You may need to do a dry run through the assembly with test-fitting so you know how the kit goes together.

Once you become thoroughly familiar with the stock kit, then you can decide just what size and style doors, windows, and exterior trim and what accessories you will want to buy in order to finish the kit to your satisfaction. You can also decide on the sequence you want to follow to

155

Fig. 12–1 Virginia Heacock added Houseworks windows and doors to the Plumbrook Cottage kit by Our House to give it a Victorian flair.

finish the kit once the basic structure is completed. But it is possible to complete most of the interior decoration on a dollhouse before devoting any time or money to finishing the exterior.

Reinforcing a Shell

One of the least expensive ways to obtain the dollhouse you desire is to purchase a ready-made plywood shell. The shell will have all of the windows and doors cut into the walls and it will be assembled and ready to detail. The plywood will tend to warp over the years, though, because there is no reinforcement of the corners and ceiling and roof joints as there is in most of the construction systems and kits. The only way to hold the shell in alignment is to make sure all the joints are *solid* before they are hidden beneath wallpaper and exterior paneling.

I suggest that you reinforce the corners and the ceiling and roof joints with white glue and join the walls with No. $8 \times 1^1/_4$-inch phillips-head woodscrews rather than with just nails. The work should be easy

Fig. 12–2 The Model Homes San Francisco Victorian House kit which can be expanded as in figure 12–3. *Courtesy Model Homes.*

Fig. 12–3 The basic house is altered considerably with the addition of Model Homes matching number 1030 Add-A-Room. *Courtesy Model Homes.*

enough if you predrill each of the screw holes with a No. 8 × 1¼-inch pilot bit in an electric drill.

If you use phillips-head screws, there is less chance of the screw head being torn by the screwdriver. The phillips-head screws are also easier to install with a *variable-speed* electric drill, if you are one of

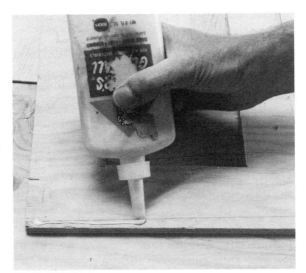

Fig. 12–4 The plywood dollhouse shells or toy dollhouses should be disassembled so that every joint can be fastened with white glue.

Fig. 12–5 Plywood dollhouse shells should also be screwed together to prevent warping. Drill a pilot hole for each screw.

those people who really like to do things the easy way. Special screwdriver bits are available for the ¼-inch and ⅜-inch electric drills. Do not try to drive screws with a conventional one-speed drill, because the drill speed is far too high.

Just before you drive the screws, run a bead of white glue down every seam. Let the glue dry for about an hour, then use a scrap of wood to scrape any excess away from the corners so that it will not interfere with installing floor paneling or wallpaper later on. (If the dollhouse is simply tacked together, you will get an even better glue joint by tearing it apart and gluing each joint as you screw it back together.)

Adapting Windows and Doors

The only "standard" sizes for dollhouse windows and doors are the sizes of the components carried by your local miniatures dealers. If you can buy it, then you can consider it to be standard. Your chances of getting windows and doors to fit the openings in your dollhouse are better if you purchase both the dollhouse and the windows and doors at the same time from the same dealer.

Some brands of windows and doors are popular enough to be considered "open stock" in many stores. You will have to let your local miniatures shop proprietor be your guide if you decide to buy new windows or doors at a later date. The door and window openings in the unfinished plywood shells sold by your local dealer should certainly match the windows and doors he or she carries in stock, but never assume that the stock will be the same two years from now.

Ready-made working windows and doors can be quite expensive, especially if you are trying to finish a house that may require twenty or more windows and several doors. You can certainly save a major proportion of the cost of ready-made windows and doors by building your own from Northeastern's milled wood shapes. That solution is also one that allows you to make virtually any size door or window so you will not have to worry about finding the proper sizes.

Never assume that you can build your own, though, until you have actually tried it. Some miniaturists find it almost as easy to build their own windows and doors as they do to install ready-built ones, while others just cannot get the hang of it no matter how hard they try. Those unfinished plywood dollhouse shells and simple kits look like there is almost nothing left to do to them, but the task of finishing them authentically can be a challenging one.

There are several ways that you can modify the openings in a dollhouse shell or kit so they will fit ready-made windows and doors. If the opening is too small, it is relatively easy to cut it larger with an electric saber saw. If you tape over the lines you will cut with masking tape and use a finishcut blade (see Chapter 2), there probably will be few splinters along the new edges. The saber saw vibrates enough to break some of the joints of an assembled house, so if your house is already built, you may have to do the cutting with a hand-held keyhole or jig saw.

It is much easier to cut the openings larger *before* the kit is assembled. If the opening is only about $1/16$ inch too small, you can enlarge it with a coarse-tooth file or even with some coarse sandpaper wrapped around a 6-inch block of 2×4 lumber.

If the opening for the door or window is only $1/8$ inch or less too large, you can glue in stripwood shims around the opening, and the

Fig. 12–6 If you are assembling a dollhouse kit, stop construction at this empty "shell" stage and install ready-made windows and doors.

shims will be hidden by the door or window frame. The shims must be no thicker than the wall if the door or window frame is to be installed properly.

Be particularly careful when you install the doors or windows that the frames are parallel with the surface of the wall. When they fit loosely or when shims are used, it is easy to install them at an angle and

Fig. 12–7 Fill small gaps around ready-made windows with strips of wood and hide the filler strips with shutters.

Fig. 12–8 The doorway was too wide for Carlson's door, so the vertical door jams were filled with ¼-inch shim strips.

Fig. 12–9 Exterior panels or Northeastern's clapboard siding can be used to hide any shims around window openings.

Fig. 12–10 Norm Nielsen added Handley House "gang-planked" hardwood floors and Houseworks windows and trim to his Dura Craft Farmhouse kit.

Fig. 12–11 Virginia Heacock added Houseworks windows and doors and AMSI Miniatures landscaping to this Willoway Farm kit by Our House.

not notice it until the glue has dried. Hold the window or door frames in place with small tacks and/or masking tape, if necessary, until the glue dries.

If the door or window is more than 1/4 inch smaller than the opening, you can still center the window or door in the opening with stripwood shims to wedge it in and use white glue to hold it in place. If the shims are visible around the frames, they can be disguised with shutters on the sides. Gaps at the top can be obscured with either ornate trim or awnings. Gaps at the bottom of windows can be hidden by flower boxes.

If you are going to cover the outside surfaces of the walls with bricks, shingles, or siding, then you will not need to worry about the shims being visible, because you can cover them with the siding. In this instance, the shims should be glued to the sides of the openings. Then the siding should be installed and the windows glued in place *after* the siding and the windows are painted.

Renovating Toy Dollhouses

I consider a "toy" dollhouse to be one constructed from plywood, pressed wood, or hardboard that is ⅛ inch or less in thickness. The walls and windows were probably punched out with a tool that resembles a cookie cutter.

If you are absolutely in love with the style of a particular toy dollhouse, then it might be worth your time to try to try to make it look as realistic as the adult dollhouses. The major problem with the toy dollhouses are the thin walls. The realistic window frames are at least ½ inch thick because that is how thick a real windowsill and molding would be if reduced to ¹/₁₂ scale.

If you try to renovate a toy dollhouse with scale-size windows, the windows will either hang too far outside the walls, or they will hang too far into the rooms. You can increase the thickness of the walls with a

Fig. 12–12 The toy-style dollhouses, such as this Celerity-brand Victorian, have punched-plywood windows and walls. *Courtesy Celerity Co.*

"system" such as Carlson's or Northeastern's, but that will be every bit as much work as building the entire house from raw materials.

The only "easy" way to improve the appearance of a toy dollhouse is to cover the exterior walls with paneling or some other material and decorate the interior walls to suit your taste.

You can leave the doors and windows alone or construct new ones, from Northeastern milled-wood shapes, to fit the thickness of the walls. The frames and sills will have to be much thinner than those in scale models, and the windows may not actually open.

It is possible, though, to capture the general feeling of a full-depth window on a $1/8$-inch wall if you are willing to build your own windows. The project will require a great deal of fitting (even if you do find some ready-built doors or windows that are the right size) because new frames must be made to fit the thinner walls.

Another possibility is worth investigating if you must have that particular style dollhouse: a local carpenter may be willing to use the thinner toy dollhouse walls as patterns and re-create the house from $1/2$-inch plywood as an unfinished shell. If you supply him with the proper ready-made windows and doors, those openings could be cut to the correct size while he cuts the shell.

The resulting plywood shell would cost several times more than the shells in the miniatures shops, but it should be much less expensive than a custom-built dollhouse.

Suppliers and Manufacturers

Your local miniatures dealer can usually provide the parts and supplies you need, order specialty catalogs for you, and answer your questions. (How to find miniatures dealers near you was discussed in Chapter 1.) But you also have the option of contacting the manufacturers directly.

Most of the firms listed below can supply catalogs of their products, but there is often a charge for them. If you write to any of these miniatures supply firms for the price of their catalog or for any other information, enclose a stamped, self-addressed envelope to assure a reply. (You might also mention where you read or heard of the firm's existence—they often like to know.)

Many of these firms are part-time businesses operated by hobbyists, and others are divisions of much larger corporations, so it may take a while for a reply to reach you.

AHM: Associated Hobby Manufacturers
   (see Woodland Scenics)
   Landscaping Materials

AMSI Miniatures
P.O. Box 750638
Petaluma, CA 94975
   Landscaping Materials

Americolor (see New England Hobby
   Supply's "Builder's Choice" paints)

Bachmann Brothers, Inc. (see Woodland
   Scenics)
   Landscaping Materials

Batrie Corporation (see Houseworks)
   Dollhouse kits and shadowboxes

California Model Co.
1426 Ritchey #A
Santa Ana, CA 92705
   Miter box

Carlson's Miniatures (see Northeastern
   Scale Models)
   Dollhouse kits, systems, and components

The Celerity Company
8635 267th St.
W. Farmington, MN 55024
   Dollhouse kits

167

Chrysolite, Inc. (see Dee's Delights)
Lamps and lighting fixtures

Cir-Kit Concepts, Inc.
407 14th St., N.W.
Rochester, MN 55901
Wiring systems, lamps, and fixtures

Con Cor, division of JMC International
1025 Industrial Drive
Bensenville, IL 60106
Imports Preiser

Craft Products Miniatures
P.O. Box 688
St. Charles, IL 60174
Solid brass hardware

Dee's Delights, Inc.
3150 State Line Rd.
Cincinnati, OH 45052
Dollhouse kits, furniture, lights, and components

Dremel Manufacturing Co.
4915 21st St.
Racine, WI 53130
Power saws and motor tools

Dura-Craft, Inc. (see Greenleaf)
Dollhouse kits

Elect-A-Lite
742-B East Arctic Ave.
Santa Maria, CA 93454
Wiring systems, lamps, and fixtures

Evergreen Scale Models
12808 Northeast 125th Way
Kirkland, WA 98034
Clear and white sheet styrene

E-Z-Lectric (see Dee's Delights, Cir-Kit, or Elect-A-Lite)
Wiring systems, lamps, and fixtures

Fantasy Dollhouses
1145 F Baker St.
Costa Mesa, CA 92626
Dollhouse interior and exterior components

Fantasy House Construction Co. (see Kimberly)
Wall surfaces and components

Floquil–Polly S Color Corporation
Route 30 North
Amsterdam, NY 12010
Paints

Carl Goldberg Models, Inc.
4734 West Chicago Ave.
Chicago, IL 60651
Super Jet cyanoacrylate cement

Greenleaf
58 No. Main St.
Honeoye Falls, NY 14472
Dollhouse kits

Handley House
P.O. Box 8658
Fort Worth, TX 76124
Dollhouse systems and components

Holgate & Reynolds
1000 Central Ave.
Wilmette, IL 60091
Metal detail castings

Houseworks, Inc.
2388 Pleasantdale Rd.
Atlanta, GA 30340
Windows, doors, bricks, and components

Illinois Hobbycrafts (see Dee's Delights)
Wiring systems, lamps, and fixtures

Kimberly House Miniatures
2935 Industrial Rd.
Las Vegas, NV 89109
Bricks, mortar, stucco, and roofing materials

L. Kummerow (see Miniaturelite)
Custom-built lamps and fixtures

Life-Like Products, Inc.
1600 Union Ave.
Baltimore, MD 21211
Landscaping materials

Lil Crafts (see Kimberly)

Masterpiece Museum Miniatures
P.O. Drawer 5280
Austin, TX 78763
  Cast-plaster miniature people

Maxwell House Miniatures (see Houseworks)
  Doors, windows, and components

Mel's Miniatures (see Houseworks and
  Dee's Delights)
  Door and window kits

Metal Miniatures (see Holgate &
  Reynolds)

Microscale
1555 Placentia
Newport Beach, CA 92663
  Plastic cement and decal products

Midwest Products Co.
400 So. Indiana St.
Hobart, IN 46342
  Dollhouse systems and wood materials

Miniaturelite
P.O. Box 164
Hinsdale, IL 60521
  Wiring systems, lamps, and fixtures

Mini Brick and Stone Co. (see Kimberly)
  Scale-model brick and stone products

Model Homes (see Greenleaf or Dee's
  Delights)
  Dollhouse kits and paints

Mueller Miniatures (see Dee's Delights)

New England Hobby Supply
71 Hilliard St.
Manchester, CT 06040
  Builder's Choice paints
  *Tools, assembly / gluing jigs, and com-
  ponents*

Norm's Dollhouses
6564 So. Broadway
Littleton, CO 80121
  *Dollhouses, shadowboxes, and com-
  ponents*

Northeastern Scale Models, Inc.
Box 727
Methuen, MA 80121
  *Dollhouse systems, doors, windows, and
  components*

Our House (see Houseworks)

Pactra Coatings, a division of Plasti-Kote
  Co., Inc.
6200 Cochran Rd.
Solon, OH 44139
  Paints

Plaid Enterprises (see Houseworks, Dee's
  Delights and New England Hobby
  Supply)
  Dollhouse kits, systems, and paints

Polly S (see Floquil)

Preiser (see Con Cor)

Real Good Toys
10 Quarry Hill
Varre, VT 05641
  Dollhouse kits

Real Life (see Scientific Models)

S/W Crafts (see Dee's Delights)
  Dollhouse kits, brick and stone kits

Doreen Sinnett Designs (see Dee's
  Delights)
  Brick sheets, furniture

Scientific Models, Inc.
340 Snyder Ave.
Berkeley Heights, NJ 07922
  Furniture kits

Sanders (see Dee's Delights)

Skil-Craft, a division of Monogram
  Models, Inc.
P.O. Box 317
Morton Grove, IL 60053
  Dollhouse kits

E. Suydam and Co. (see California Model
  Co.)
  Miter box tool

Testor Corporation
620 Buckbee St.
Rockford, IL 61104
Paints and glues

Woodland Scenics
P.O. Box 98
Linn Creek, MO 65052
Landscaping materials

Wilson Works (see Norm's Dollhouses)
Shadowbox kits

Woodline (see Norm's Dollhouses)
Shadowboxes

Wood Works (see New England Hobby
  Supply)
Assembly/gluing jigs

Index

Page numbers in **bold** refer to illustrations.

Aluminum downspouts and gutters, 80
American Life Foundation & Study Institute, 151, **153,** 154
AMSI Miniatures, **86,** 89, 91–93, **91, 92, 164**
Austin, Cecil Boyd, figurine painted by, 123, **123**

Base. *See* Plywood base
Batrie Dollhouses, **150, 151**
Blacksmith shop diorama, **111,** 115
Board and batten siding, 69, 71
Brads, in wiring operation, 50, 51
Bricks
  applying, 57–62, **60**
  cutting, **60,** 64
  cutting openings in sheets of, 58–59
  painting panels of, 62–63
  real scale-model, 63–64
  simplified, 64–67
  weathered or aged, **61,** 63

Cardboard, windows and doors in, 26–28
Carl Goldberg Models, 40
Carlson system, **3,** 144, **146–148, 162**
Carpenter's combination square, 22
Carpets, 42–43
Ceilings in shadowboxes, 106–107
Cement. *See also* Glue
  contact, for applying siding, 59, 61
  cyanoacrylate, 38, 40
Chimney, **66,** 80
Chrysolite, lamp of, **45**
Cir-Kit units, **45,** 46, **47,** 50–51, **50, 124**

Clapboard siding, 67–69
Claudon, Charles, dioramas by, 112, 113, **114–117,** 116–117, 119, 123
Color transparencies, techniques for using, **124–126,** 126, 129–132
Concrete effects, 86, 88
Copper roofing material, 78, 80
Copper-tape wiring systems, 49–52
Costs of building miniatures, 14, 16–18
Cutting
  brick sheets, openings in, 58–59
  bricks, **60,** 64
  cardboard, 27, **27**
  door openings, 21–22, **23, 24,** 25, 58–59, 160
  foam, 89
  foam-core board, 26, 27, **27, 145**
  glass, 32
  molding and coping, **39,** 40
  plastic, 27, **27**
  plywood, 25
  shingles, 74, **75**
  slice-and-break technique for, **145**
  splinter-free, **23,** 25, **153**
  styrene and Plexiglas sheets, **145**
  thin sheetwood wall panels, **153**
  tools for, 22, **24,** 25, **152**
  wainscoting, **39,** 40
  window openings, 21–22, **23, 24,** 25, 58–59, 160
  X or diagonal, 27, **27**

Diagonal-cut technique, 27, **27**

171

Dick, Betty, dioramas made by, **100,** 113, **117, 118,** 119
Diorama, 10–14. *See also* Shadowbox dioramas
Dirt in landscaping, 90–91
Dollhouses, 139–166
 building from plans, 148, 150–151, 154
 cost of building, 14, 16–18
 differentiated from dioramas, 10–14
 plywood shell system of construction of, 147–148
 quick-build kits and systems for, 139–154
 renovation of, 155–166
Dolls, 120–126
Doors and windows, 21–32
 adapting, to interiors, 30
 assembly of, 29
 in brick or stone exterior, 58
 in cardboard, 26–28
 cutting openings for, 21–25, 58–59, 160
 fitting in oversize holes, 160, 164
 fitting in undersize holes, 160
 in foam-core board, 26, 27
 handles and locks for, 30
 installation of, 30–32
 in plywood, 25–26
 renovation of, 160–164
 upgrading with better-quality, 17
Dormers, 80–83
Downspouts, 80
Dremel Manufacturing Co., saw by, **152**

E-Z-Lectric wiring system, **53,** 54
Electrical wiring, 44–54
 conventional, installing, 52, 54
 for lights and lamps, 46–47
 systems of, 44–49
 tape-and-punch, 49–52
 three-step, 50–51, **51, 52**
 turns in, 50–51
Endlich, Eve, garden scene by, **129,** 132
Evergreen, plastic strips of, 78

Fantasy House, slate shingles by, 76
Fences, 86
Figures. *See* Dolls
Fireplaces, making brick, **66**
Flecto's Varathane, 41, 43
Flocking, applying, 90
Floors, 40–43
Floquil's stain, **28**
Foam, rigid, in landscaping, 89, 93
Foam-core board, 26, 27, **103, 143,** 144, **145**
Foam rubber, ground, 91, 92
Foliage, 88–89
Frames, **35,** 102–106
Furniture, 8, 9

Gang-planking, 40–42
Glass, installing window, 32
Glue(ing). *See also* Cement
 of exterior siding, 61, 63–64
 of flooring, 41
 of foliage, 93, 95
 for metal, 80
 of wallpaper, 36, **37**
 of windows, 38, **38**
Grass, simulating, 89–91
Ground cover, 89–91
Gutters, 80

Handley House
 dollhouse construction system, 144
 foam-core Mini-Board, **103,** 26, 27, **143,** 144, **145**
 gang-planking, 40–41, **40, 163**
 shingles, 74, **76**
 siding, **62, 63,** 67, 68
 Spanish tiles, **77,** 78
Heacock, Virginia, dollhouse by, **164**
Holgate & Reynolds, brick panels by, **59**
Houseworks
 bricks, **60,** 64
 dollhouse construction system, **7, 163, 164**
 doors by, **28**

Infinity box, 130–135

Kits and systems, 139–155

L. Kummerow, strip metal by, 119
Lamps, 44–49
Lancaster, Pete, dollhouse by, **7**
Landscaping, 84–95
 concrete effects, 86, 88
 ground cover, 89–91
 lawn and foliage, 88–89
 porches and patios, 85–86
 trees and shrubs, 91–95
 yard, 84–85
Lawn, 88–89
Lighting, 44–49, 106–107
Lil Brics, 64–65, **65–67**
Lil Crafts, bricks and mortar by, 64, 65
Linoleum, 42–43
Lintels, 58
Liquitape, 36, **37**
Lundquist, J.B., dollhouse of, **5**

McLeod, Joel, bricks cut by, **61,** 64
Magic Brick, 65, 67, **68**
Magic Stone, 65, 67, **69**
Masterpiece Museum Miniatures, 119, **122,** 123, **123**

Mel's Miniatures, 29, **29**
Metal Miniatures, **87,** 115
Midwest system, **39,** 68, 71, 146, **149, 153**
Milhollin, Pat, "people" by, **122,** 123
Mini-Board, 26, 27, **103, 143,** 144, **145**
Miniatures
  costs of building, 14, 16–18
  where to buy, 3–7, 167–171
Mirrors, special effects with, 132–135
Miter boxes, 40
Model Homes system, **4, 15,** 54, **82, 157, 158**
Molding, 37–40
Mortar for brick walls, 63–64, 65, 67
Mueller Miniatures, 54

Nielsen, Norm, 25, 50, **94, 130,** 132, **134, 163**
Norm's Dollhouses, **2**
Northeastern system, **7,** 29, **29,** 67–68, **70,** 71, 74, **76,** 80, **81,** 144, **149, 153, 163**
NorthWest Short Line "Chopper," **152**

Our House kits and systems, 68, 141, 143–144, **164**

Painting
  of brick and stone panels, 62–63
  for carpets and linoleum, 43
  with clear epoxy, for floors, 42
  of concrete areas, 88
  of figures, 123
  of floor, 42
  of siding, 68–69
  to simulate slate shingles, 76
  of small accessories, **35**
  for weathered effect. *See* Weathered effect
  of windows, 32
Parker, W. Oren, 111
Patios, 85–86
Peggy Nisbet collector's dolls, 125
Perspective, forced, 112–113
Photograph. *See* Color transparencies
Picture frames, painting, **35**
Plexiglas, 106, 107, **145,** 131, 132, 135
Plywood, working with, 25–26
Plywood base, **84–85**
Plywood shell system, 147–148, 156, 158–159
Porches, 85–86

Rafters, 80
Real Good Toys, **9–12**
Real Life, diorama by, **100**
Renovating, 17, 155–166
Roof. *See also* Shingles
  chimneys and downspouts for, 80
  dormers for, 80–83
  grass, 79–80
  metal, 78

  overhang of, 73–74
  pitch of, changing, 73–74, 81, 83
  thatch, 79–80
  tile, **77,** 78

Scale, 4–5, 7
Shadowbox diorama, 10–14, 99–109. *See also* Special effects; Stagecraft
  accessibility of, 107–109
  advantages and limitations of, 99–101
  cost of building, 14, 16–18
  frames for, 102–106
  as furniture, 102–103
  lighting for, 106–107
  mock-up or model of scene in planning of, 114
  one-scene, 99–109
Shakes, 74. *See also* Shingles
Shims, 160–161, 164
Shingles, 74–76
  cutting, 74, **75**
  installing, 74, **75, 76**
  plastic and paper-mache, 58
  slate, 76
  weathered effect on, 74, **75, 76**
Shiplap siding, 67–69, **70**
Shrubs, 91–95
Sidewalls, in forced perspective, 112–113
Siding, 57–72. *See also* Brick
  applying, 57–62
  board-and-batten, 69, 71, **71**
  clapboard and other wood, 67–69, **70**
  painting, 62–63, 68–69
  stucco effects, 71–72
Sills, 30, 58
Skil-Craft dollhouse kits, **17**
Slate shingles, 76
Smith, Harvey K., 111
Spanish tiles, **77,** 78
Special effects, 120–135
  dolls, 120–126
  "infinity box," 130–135
  with mirrors, 132–133
  rear-projection window scenes, 126, 129–132
Sprayment, 3M, 36, **37**
Stagecraft, 110–119. *See also* Special effects
  examples of, 113, 115, **115–118,** 116, 119
  forced perspective in, 112–113
  model or mock-up in, 114–115
  set-design basics for, 110–111
Stone
  applying exterior, 58
  cutting opening in sheets of, 58–59
  painting panels of, 62–63
  simplified, 64–67
Stucco finish, 71–72
S/W Crafts, **6,** 65, 67, 68, **68, 69, 140**

Tape-and-punch wiring, 49–52
Testor's Dullcote, 43
Testor's Glosscote, 43
Tiles, Spanish, **77,** 78
Tools, **8,** 22, **24,** 25, **152**
Transparencies. *See* Color transparencies
Trees, 91–95

Varnish, floor, 41

Wainscoting, 37–40
Wallpaper, self-stick, 36, **37**
Walls
    exterior. *See* Brick; Siding
    interior, 33–40
    molding and wainscoting, 37–40
    paints for interior, 33–36
    self-stick wallpaper for, 36, **37**
Weathered effects
    for brick, **61,** 63

for shingles, 74, **75, 76**
on shiplap boards, 68
for Spanish tile, **77,** 78
Wilmoite, Peggy Helm, home built by, **79**
Wilson, Fred, 100–101, **101, 111,** 115
Wilson Works, 100, **101, 113, 118**
Window frames, exterior, 57–59
Window scenes, 126, 129–132
Windows. *See* Doors and windows
Wiring, electrical. *See* Electrical wiring
Wood siding, 67–69. *See also* Plywood
Wood Works, **30**
Woodland Scenics, 92
Woodline system, **15, 28,** 68, **75, 104, 105, 108,**
    140–141, **141, 142**

X-Acto shadowbox, **100**
X-cut technique, 27, **27**

Yard area, 84–85